Journalling the Bible

Published by
The Bible Reading Fellowship
15 The Chambers, Vineyard
Abingdon OX14 3FE
United Kingdom
Tel: +44 (0)1865 319700
Email: enquiries@brf.org.uk
Website: www.brf.org.uk
BRF is a Registered Charity

ISBN 978 1 84101 736 5
First published 2014
10 9 8 7 6 5 4 3 2 1 0

Acknowledgments

Unless otherwise stated, scripture quotations are taken from The Holy Bible,
New International Version (Anglicised edition) copyright © 1979, 1984, 2011
by Biblica. Used by permission of Hodder & Stoughton Publishers, an Hachette
UK company. All rights reserved. 'NIV' is a registered trademark of Biblica. UK
trademark number 1448790.

Scripture quotations from The New Revised Standard Version of the Bible,
Anglicised edition, copyright © 1989, 1995 by the Division of Christian Education
of the National Council of the Churches of Christ in the United States of America,
are used by permission. All rights reserved.

Scripture quotations from the Good News Bible published by The Bible Societies/
HarperCollins Publishers Ltd, UK © American Bible Society 1966, 1971, 1976,
1992, used with permission.

Scripture quotations from THE MESSAGE. Copyright © by Eugene H. Peterson 1993,
1994, 1995. Used by permission of NavPress Publishing Group.

Extracts from the Authorised Version of the Bible (The King James Bible), the
rights in which are vested in the Crown, are reproduced by permission of the
Crown's Patentee, Cambridge University Press.

p. 58: This copyright prayer is taken from *A New Zealand Prayer Book – He Karakia
Mihinare o Aotearoa* and is used with permission from The Anglican Church in
Aotearoa, New Zealand and Polynesia.

Cover image: Gabriele Maltinti/Shutterstock

A catalogue record for this book is available from the British Library

Printed and bound by CPI Group (UK) Ltd, Croydon CR0 4YY

Journalling the Bible

40 writing exercises

Corin Child

Contents

Foreword

I started my first journal on 11 November 1992. How can I remember the exact date? Well, it was the day that the Church of England's General Synod voted to allow women to become priests for the very first time. It was especially significant for me because I was in the second year of my ordination training in Durham, and I'd begun my training without knowing when, if ever, I would be able to be ordained to the priesthood.

When the vote went through, I was so overwhelmed that the only way I could make sense of what was happening was to open the front cover of a pristine hardback notebook and to write—and write, and write, and write.

Since then, I've added to that notebook, and many others besides, over 21 years of ministry. When times have been good, I've celebrated by writing about them. When times have been tough, I've found consolation and meaning in setting down my thoughts on paper. It's only when reading back over 20 years' worth of journals that I can see so clearly God's hand in my life, prompting, steadying, guiding.

In this practical and stimulating book, Corin Child shares the fruits of many years of spiritual journalling. He encourages us to write in response to that blockbuster set of journals we call the Bible, and in so doing to learn more about ourselves and the God who guides and shapes our lives. Whether you are new to journalling or an old hand, used to writing alone or prompted to try it in a group setting, this book will be a trusted, insightful and inspiring companion on your journey.

The Venerable Jan McFarlane, Archdeacon of Norwich

Introduction

Why journalling?

This is a book of reflections with a difference. It contains selected passages from the Bible and reflections on those passages, but it suggests that, rather than simply reading and thinking in response, you do some journalling too. Why? Because, as many journal keepers will tell you, there is something in the practice of writing things down that is good for the soul.

Think for a moment of some of the ways that people are helped by writing things down. When mathematicians write down problems, an equation becomes easier to work through. When students compose essays, they prove to their tutor and to themselves that they have understood history or politics. When busy parents write shopping lists, they remember to pick up milk in the supermarket even while the children are distracting them. When someone retires and writes a memoir, they discover just how many memories they have.

A Christian who keeps a journal does all of these things in some measure. Journalling can work through the problems and paradoxes of our lives and of faith. Journalling consolidates the things we know and believe. Journalling sets down things that we want to hold on to for later. Journalling finds things buried deep inside us and brings them to the surface.

Christians attribute all sorts of spiritual benefits to their journal writing. Some talk of their journal as an 'Ebenezer', recalling 1 Samuel 7:12, where recording milestones allows the journal keeper to say, 'Thus far the Lord has helped us'. Others note the advice of Socrates that 'the unexamined life is not worth living' and its biblical counterparts, such as Psalm 139:1 and Psalm 103:2, and say that journalling is a way of savouring daily experience rather than blindly letting it rush past. The writer Ron Klug lists ten potential benefits of spiritual journalling, including better decision-making, release of emotions and goal-setting for the future.[1]

Our everyday consciousness easily becomes confused, harried, fretful and forgetful. In these circumstances, a journal can be exactly what we need. The few rough notes we have been keeping suddenly become a bridge to a steadier frame of mind. A dog-eared journal with loose leaves and coffee stains on the cover may not seem very valuable to the casual observer, but to its owner it is a sanctuary and a treasury.

Why the Bible?

'In the Bible, history is God's biography.'[2] The Bible is, in effect, a journal on a grand scale. Although it has many authors and encompasses many different types of writing, scripture has a common purpose: to set down what God has done and to help us understand how people have responded. The book of Psalms preserves poetry about the highs and lows of living with faith. The Gospels journal the ministry of Jesus (and, in John 20:31, the author is quite clear about the purpose of his record). Israel's historians detailed the prosperity and ruin of God's people. The epistles of the early church are letters worth keeping.

Since the Bible has this connection with journal-keeping, it is a good place to find patterns for our own journalling. With its assortment of genres, scripture demonstrates that spiritual records can also be creative and varied in style. This book suggests 40 exercises, each arising from a Bible passage. My hope is that, by getting under the skin of scripture, by sensing the exhilaration of the psalmist, the evangelist, the chronicler and the apostle, you will be stirred to write after their example. You could say that journalling is an entirely natural response to reading the Bible.

One of the thrilling things to discover here is that the content of the Bible is not just instructive; it is inspiring. The Bible is rarely the monotone teacher who sits behind the desk; it is more often the tousle-haired enthusiast who leaps around the classroom waving his arms. This is because its writers cared deeply about what they were putting across. They wanted the recipients of their message to be moved. Romans, for instance, is often thought of as a book of theological doctrines. Read parts of it aloud, however, and you realise that it was written with considerable flair. Romans 8 has all the cadences of a Churchillian speech, and suggests a way for today's readers to begin journalling about their own cherished beliefs. (You will find Romans 8 featured in Reflection 26, 'Credal crescendo'.)

Journalling with this book

The 40 reflections begin with Genesis and move through different books of the Bible. There are Old Testament passages in the first half, New Testament passages in the second, and reflections on the Psalms interspersed. The Bible passage is where each reflection starts and is followed by some thoughts on the theme, a journalling exercise and some follow-up activities. Here are some further things to think about as you use this book.

- **Using this book during Lent:** Since there are 40 reflections, one of the intended uses is as a Lent resource. The reflections are arranged in groups of six (four for the week that starts with Ash Wednesday), meaning that there is a passage for each weekday and a psalm for the weekend. The concluding reflections focus on Jesus' trial and crucifixion in John's Gospel; these are suitable for Holy Week.
- **Using this book at other times of the year:** It is equally possible to use the exercises at a different time of the year, or to dip into them from time to time. It doesn't matter if you don't do the exercises in order. Indeed, you might like to skip to a more upbeat or a more ponderous reflection according to the mood you find yourself in.
- **Finding a time of day for your journalling:** As with any regular engagement with the Bible, you may find it helpful to set aside a certain time of day for your journalling. First thing in the morning and last thing at night are the two obvious choices. One will 'set you up for the day'; the other will 'write the day behind you'. If you can be flexible, however, then note that certain exercises are suited to a particular time of day. For example, Reflection 32, 'Imagine how it will go', anticipates the day ahead, while Reflection 12, 'Less is blessed', talks about writing in an 'evening mood'.
- **Choosing where you will do your journalling:** The question of what you will write with and where you will write are connected. If you prefer the tactile experience of pen and paper, it makes sense to set up a desk in a quiet room or identify the place where you will be most comfortable journalling. If you do everything on a computer or a tablet, then do your journalling electronically. However, you probably won't want emails and notifications distracting

you while you think, write and pray, so give this some thought; and if you generally use your device in a busy or cluttered area, you may need to move somewhere quieter while you journal. You might like to vary the place where you journal from time to time; for instance, Reflection 22, 'Inside and out', suggests going outside to see what is going on in God's world.

- **Including creative writing in your journal:** 'I had my breakfast, went to work, and came home' is one kind of journal entry but it is not an imaginative one. Journalling can be much more inventive than this, and can spill over into creative writing. Just as the Bible communicates with different types of poetry and rhetoric, so it is possible to record the spiritual and emotional content of your day using different forms of writing. Using a particular idiom is integral to certain journalling exercises in this book; for instance, Reflection 2, 'The beauty of benediction', suggests that you write a blessing after the example of Numbers 6. In other journalling exercises, an idea for creative writing is included as a supplement. For instance, in Reflection 37, 'Epigrams of doubt and faith', the main exercise asks you to journal different voices in the world around you; you then have the option of turning these opinions into a scripted conversation. Creative writing of this sort can be enjoyable and may provide something interesting to share with other people, whether in a journalling group or as an online post.
- **Reviewing what you have written:** Going back even just a few days in your journal, to see what you were thinking then and what has changed since, is one of the ways that journalling can break our preoccupation with the present and give us perspective. Of course, you can do this when-

ever you like, but you could make a point of doing so regularly if, for instance, you are following this book through Lent. You might review your journal at the end of every week, giving thanks for any answered prayers or personal progress. If you are journalling more sporadically, you could review your journal at natural intervals in your life, such as during holidays or at the start or end of a certain season.

- **Writing in private and sharing your journal:** As far as your journal is concerned, privacy must be possible. You need to be able to write what you really think without having the thought in the back of your mind, 'What if someone reads this?' There are various things you can do to ensure privacy: the simplest is to explain to the people who live with you that your journal is just for you. If you journal on a tablet or computer, password protection can be a useful feature.

   Although spiritual journalling begins with you and God, the result of creating something can often be an impulse to share it (perhaps to the author's surprise). Ways of sharing your work include blogging or social networking, contributing to parish or community magazines or simply showing your writing to those around you. Reflection 10, 'Hymns private and public', discusses the balance between sharing your journal and keeping it personal.

Journalling in a group

As well as being used individually, these reflections can be used as a group resource. If you have a number of people who like journalling or who are at least prepared to try it, you will find that writing together can be a rewarding way into discussing faith and building fellowship with each other. Here are a few suggestions for running a group:

Introducing people to the idea

Journalling in a group will be a novel idea to many (it may be to you). A good way of developing some enthusiasm is to give people a taste of what is involved. Choose one of the 40 reflections and invite people to an introductory meeting where you go through the material together. There is a unique group dynamic that comes from sitting, writing and sharing together, and when people have experienced this, they may be keen for more.

It is possible to incorporate this sort of taster session into a church service or even a sermon. You should heed the necessary logistics, such as how people will get access to pens and paper, and how to include those (including children) who may have difficulty in writing. If you use one of the passages in this book as the theme of the service, you may be surprised at how engaged people become if they are allowed to respond to God through journalling rather than letting the preacher do all the work.

If you already belong to any kind of fellowship group, you can arrange for everyone to try journalling at one of your meetings. One of the benefits of journalling before you discuss a Bible passage is that people will have time to think about their response, and everyone, not just the loud ones, will have something they can share.

A further way of attracting people is to give the group a specific purpose. A gathering of Christians from different churches observing Lent together would be an example.

Setting up a group

Give some thought to the venue for your group; certain places will give the group a certain atmosphere. Will your group members prefer a home with a log fire, a lively coffee shop or a cathedral cloister? It will probably help to have a regular venue, but you don't have to stick to it. If you think ahead, you can arrange some 'away days' where you use a particular journalling session in a location with a fitting feel. This is certainly worth considering when you get to the reflections on John's Gospel (which you may be using during Holy Week): consider journalling in a church or in view of a cross.

Give some thought to how often you will meet, how long each meeting will last and how many meetings you intend to have in total. Once you know this, you can work out which of the reflections you are going to use and in what order. If, for example, you are going to meet for an hour and a half once a week in Lent, then you might use two reflections per meeting (giving each one 45 minutes), using a mixture of Old and New Testament passages.

Using the material

A basic template for a group meeting is as follows:

- Read the passage and the reflection that accompanies it.
- Spend some time journalling quietly.
- Reconvene to share and discuss what people have written.

The 'Share' section for each day suggests how you can tailor the material for use within a group, and you will often be able to use the 'Go further' section together as well. At the end of each meeting, briefly plan ahead. Look at the 'Share' and 'Go further' sections in the material you are going to use next time, as there may be things to prepare in advance.

The material for each day

Whether you are journalling individually or as a group, each reflection has several sections for you to work through. Here is a quick guide.

- **Read:** Find the passage for the day and read it attentively. You may like to record your first thoughts on the passage in your journal before you go any further (see the journalling template on page 18).
- **Consider:** The concern of this section is to point out the passion and the genius of each passage. In many cases there are comparisons with other inspiring works, such as famous diaries, literature, song writing, film or television. Here you can find out how Samuel Pepys resembles the psalmist, how C.S. Lewis is the cousin of Jonah, and what James Bond can reveal about the Acts of the Apostles. The aim is to illustrate various motifs found in the Bible and echoed elsewhere, which can prompt your own creative journalling.
- **Write:** The next step is to respond with some writing of your own, and this section gives a journalling exercise to help you connect the Bible passage with your own experience. You don't need to write a lot; you don't need to finish the exercise; you don't even need to follow the instructions if you prefer to journal in a different direction. But it is worth putting some time aside for unhurried contemplation and creativity.

- **Share:** As well as providing ideas for journalling groups, this section occasionally suggests how you can make connections with your circle of friends if you are following the material individually. Also, some group activities can be adapted for individual use, so have a look at this section even if you are journalling alone.
- **Go further:** This section signposts parts of the Bible and cultural excerpts that are related to the theme of the reflection, which may be of interest. (A great many of the poems, songs, paintings and works of literature mentioned here can be found online.) The practices of journal keeping and Bible reading can trigger associations with the world we live in; here you can begin to follow your thoughts in various directions.
- **A note on the passage:** The Bible is a fascinating book and some of the reflections mention a further detail in the passage that invites comment or holds a lesson for journalling.

A journalling template

Below is a template to show how you can lay out your journalling as you work through this book. On the following page you will find an example of a completed template based on reflection 1, 'And God said...', written by an imaginary journal-keeper called Anne.

Reflection:	Reading:
My own thoughts on the passage:	
Journalling exercise	
Other things I am thinking and praying about today:	Things to revisit later:

Reflection:	Reading:
1: And God said...	*Genesis 1*

My own thoughts on the passage:

Reading this passage makes me think of arguments people sometimes have about whether the world was made in 7 days or not. On the other hand, verse 22 ('let the birds increase on the earth') reminds me of the flock of starlings I saw yesterday evening.

I've always liked the line 'And God saw that it was good.'

Journalling exercise

New things that are happening in my life:

And God said, 'Let there be a new place for Anne to live; a new house in a new town.' And so I moved out of the house I have lived in for 10 years, and here I am living in a town centre for the first time!

And God said, 'Let there be people for Anne to meet.' And it was so. Everyone seems lovely at work so far. (Not sure about the boss—is he grumpy every day?)

And God said, 'Let Anne come across a book about journalling and become interested in the idea.' So here I am, giving it a go.

Other things I am thinking and praying about today:	Things to revisit later:
Thinking about all the things I've got to get done—reports that need finishing, several birthday presents to buy.	*It will be interesting to see how accurate my first impressions of my boss are...*
Praying for Jean in hospital and David starting college.	*Have been thinking about the question in 'Go further'—what do I hope to get out of my journalling? I hope it will make me calmer and maybe a bit more prayerful. We'll see!*

How this book came to be written

I have journalled for most of my adult life, not in any spectacularly organised way but simply when I felt an urge to do so. Often it has been a way of dealing with new circumstances, such as changing jobs or reaching a certain birthday. I have also kept journals through retreats and conferences, and found that the result was not only a record of events but a way of settling matters in my mind.

Then a few years ago I wrote a booklet about how creative writing can be used in a church setting.[3] One of the possibilities I explored was the idea of creative journalling and, having written about it, I decided that this was something I wanted to do more of myself. I discovered that by writing poems, ditties, prayers and even short stories in my journal, I was expressing myself in a more concentrated way. When I review these journal entries, I prefer them to pages of facts about what happened during the day; they are a better record of what has been going on in my spirit.

At the same time as the booklet was published, I became involved with the Association of Christian Writers (ACW), for whom I have led a number of writing workshops. I find them rewarding: there is so much good humour when a group (even a group of strangers) develops a writing idea and opens up to one another. After a writing workshop at the Christian Resources Exhibition, where we used Bible passages as a starting point for our own writing, I was asked to write a regular column called 'Finding inspiration' for ACW's magazine, *Christian Writer*. Those columns formed the starting point for this book.

The writing of every book has its own story and, in this case, its own set of coincidences, arising from the fact that, while writing, I have been getting on with parish ministry and everyday living. For example, while I was writing the reflection entitled 'The freedom of finding you're foolish', I turned up for a clergy cricket match two weeks early—which made me feel foolish. While writing 'Less is blessed', a reflection about being sparing with words, I attended a long funeral that included too many speeches. While writing 'A moment of ease', I had a long pastoral conversation with somebody who needed, more than anything, a break from a stressful situation. The irony was tangible as I wrote 'A tangle with time' with a looming deadline for submitting the manuscript.

I have been looking closely at the Bible while developing the material, and this has made me aware of many interesting details. After writing 'Lions, bulls, dogs and a worm', for instance, I began to notice just how often the Bible's authors make comparisons with animals to understand people: they clearly had beastly imaginations! Once I had written the reflection on Genesis 1, I noticed how much creating God continues to do—for instance in Psalm 51:10 and Isaiah 43:15 (where the same distinctive Hebrew word for 'create' occurs). In listening to the tone of the Bible's 'journalling', I was struck by the general sense of yearning in the Old Testament and the sense of optimism in the New.

All in all, I feel that I have lived through these Bible passages and these reflections as I have gone along. I hope very much that, as you journal the Bible, you will experience something similar.

1

And God said...

Read: Genesis 1

And God said, 'Let there be light.' ... And God said,
'Let the water teem with living creatures.' ... And God said,
'Let the land produce living creatures' (vv. 3, 20, 24).

Consider

Ask a Bible reader for some memorable words from the book's opening, and they might well plump for 'In the beginning'. These have a certain gravitas, which is perhaps why John commandeered them for the opening of his Gospel. As for the rest of the chapter—well, God makes some stuff, and it's all very nice.

But when was the last time you really *read* Genesis 1? Sit down with it, take it in slowly, and you can't fail to be impressed by the wonder it communicates. The divine artist gives shade, shape and substance to the empty universal space—not with chisels or brushes, but with simple words as clear as air or water. If you want some truly memorable words from this chapter, I suggest 'And God said' (or their equivalent in different translations). These are the words that mark each movement of creation, that repeat like the beating of a heart.

Edgar Allen Poe defined poetry as 'the rhythmical creation

of beauty',[4] and there is surely something poetic in the rhythm of Genesis 1. It is a passage that introduces us to a God who creates with the regularity of a new day dawning. He names his plans and they happen, true to his word. Having read the chapter, the question you might ask is 'Was that it?' Christians would answer—no, God loves his creation, and he is involved with it every day.

Write

What has God said since this first creation? What beauty, what growth, what progress did God voice at the beginning of *this* day? As a journalling exercise, begin with the words 'And God said', and write about something new that is happening. Perhaps you are aware of fresh themes in your life; perhaps you can think of a series of recent events that worked out beautifully. Use 'And God said' to create a rhythm in your writing; imagine what God has declared and what has resulted, after the fashion of Genesis 1.

As you begin journalling, it may be helpful to refer to the template on page 18 and the example of a completed template that uses this journalling exercise (page 19).

Share

When you have completed a journalling exercise, there are various things you can do with it. If you prefer to keep your work to yourself, keep it in a notebook or journal or store it electronically so that you can revisit it at a later date. If you are inclined to share something you have written, look out for opportunities (see the Introduction for suggestions about who might be interested).

If you are following these exercises as part of a journalling group, read some of what you have written to each other. As members of your group share what they believe God is currently creating, you will probably learn a fair bit about each other's lives and faith.

Go further

- Find some poetry that contemplates God's creation (there is plenty on the internet). 'Nature's hymn to the deity' by John Clare and 'Immanence' by Evelyn Underhill are a good start (notice how these poems use rhythm and repeating patterns as they relate God's creativity).
- If you are journalling at the beginning of Lent, spend some time thinking and praying about how you might grow spiritually during the coming weeks. Look at some passages that celebrate God's regular inner renewing, such as 2 Corinthians 4:16 and 5:17. Write down your hopes for Lent or for your journalling generally.

2

The beauty of benediction

Read: Numbers 6:22–26

'The Lord turn his face toward you...' (v. 26).

Consider

The best gifts do not always cost money, as children and parents sometimes discover. 'Look, I made something for you,' one of the family will say as they offer a present. It might be a home-made card, or some crêpe paper jewellery, or a thrown-together cake. As long as it is hand-crafted and tailor-made, a gift like this will always convey a kind heart.

In the book of Numbers, God gives his people certain rites and regulations, but in a touching passage at the end of chapter 6, he gives them something else that stands out. It is the 'Aaronic benediction', a carefully crafted, tailor-made form of words. The priests and leaders of Israel will use the benediction to extend blessings and the warmth of God's heart to all the people.

The three verses of the benediction are wonderfully harmonious. In Hebrew the first verse is three words, the second is five words, and the third is seven words (made up of twelve, 14 and 16 syllables respectively). Even in translation, their rising and resounding brightness can be clearly heard, which is why they are used internationally in Christian worship as well as in traditional Jewish ritual. It is a simple picture: God's countenance is turned towards and shining upon those he loves, and it culminates in *shalom*, the pervasive goodness and peace that only God can give.

Write

For your journal entry today, write a blessing of your own. You may not arrive at something as timeless as the prescribed words in Numbers 6, but you can make it heartfelt, and you can use the Aaronic benediction as a pattern.

Decide whom you would like to bless. This is worth thinking through for a moment. Should it be a friend in need? A group of people? Or even someone who is causing you trouble (remembering Jesus' sanction that we should pray for those who persecute us)? Keep your blessing simple but give it structure (perhaps making each line a little longer than the one before, which makes the sound swell). Try to make your blessing 'resound' so that the words echo with your good wishes. You could read your blessing aloud and spend a moment in prayer afterwards.

Share

You should feel free to keep the words you have written between you and God, but in some cases it may be appropriate to pass on what you have written. A simple blessing, neatly written and graciously given, could be a great encouragement to a hard-pressed friend or colleague.

If you are writing in a group, talk about how you have encountered spoken blessings. Are they used in one-to-one situations or in public worship? Are there ways that you could use blessings in your fellowship that you haven't thought of before?

Once you have done the journalling exercise, go round the group sharing what you have written and why, but agree that anyone in the group may 'pass' without any need to explain why. There may be strong feelings involved, or it may simply seem right to dwell quietly on something.

Go further

• Look up other blessings and doxologies in the Bible: Psalm 67 and Jude 24–25 are two to start with. Identify the phrases and images that you particularly like, so that you increase your appreciation of these good words.

A note on the passage

What exactly is going on when someone pronounces a blessing? 'The Lord bless you and keep you' is surely more than just a kind wish, but it is not exactly a prayer either, since it is addressed to a congregation rather than to God. There is a heartfelt force in these words, which God is behind (Numbers 6:27).

The Old Testament theologian John Goldingay makes a comparison with what happens when a minister declares that a person is baptised. 'The priest's words are more than informative,' he writes. 'They are performative; they make the blessing happen. Yet they do so only because God wills to have things work this way.'[5]

3

Rock songs

Read: Deuteronomy 32:1–47

Oh, praise the greatness of our God! He is the Rock, his works are perfect, and all his ways are just (vv. 3b–4).

Consider

A good rock song needs a good image. Classic rock songs often demonstrate this in their titles, such as 'Smoke on the water', 'Purple haze' or 'Stairway to heaven'. If a songwriter uses strong images, they stimulate the mind's eye as well as the ear. (Rock songs also like to startle and confuse the other senses—for example, 'Smells like teen spirit' and 'Come on, feel the noize'.)

The original Rock song comes not from Led Zeppelin or Jimi Hendrix but from Moses. After a lifetime of leadership, struggle and faith, Moses gives the people lyrics that celebrate what a strength God is when he is recognised and what an obstruction he is when ignored. At the centre of the song is a grand image: God is 'the Rock' (vv. 4, 15, 18, 30). When compared to the flimsy deities of other nations, Moses insists, 'Their rock is not like our Rock' (v. 31).

For the imaginations of the people of Israel, the metaphor is entirely appropriate. They had been wandering among the crags of the desert. Rock would have been the strongest and most impassable stuff they had encountered. Curiously, rocks were also places where they found food, from bees' nests and olive trees (mentioned in verse 13), and the rock itself had provided life-sustaining water for them on one memorable occasion (Exodus 17:6). To compare God to a rock was to set the minds of his people bustling with memories.

Write

Using the form of a song is a tried and tested way of offering prayer and praise, and you can incorporate this form in your journal. Think of things that you have to thank God for (or perhaps things you have learned as a result of ignoring him) and journal them as simple lyrics. Choose an image from your surroundings that reminds you of God's character, and use this through your song (it might even provide you with a title). Appeal to the other senses as well if you can, just as the song of Moses does (vv. 13–14, 32–33).

Share

If you are part of a journalling group, it may be worth trying to do this exercise separately and in different places before coming together to share your thoughts. This way, you will end up with a variety of images (something written on a cliff top will probably feel different from something written in the centre of a town or city).

God is compared to a rock in various places throughout the Old Testament, and there is a parallel in the New Testament as Jesus is compared to a cornerstone (Ephesians 2:20). You could have a look at some of these passages together in a group.

Go further

- Images are still an important way of understanding God in Christian music and worship. Look at the words of 'Rock of Ages, cleft for me' by Augustus Toplady and research the story of how it came to be written.
- Which other Christian songs use a central image to describe God that you find helpful? Flick through the titles in a song book or hymn book to remind yourself.

A note on the passage

The words of modern rock songs may be whimsical or profane, but in verse 47 Moses stresses that the words he has shared are vital: 'They are not just idle words for you—they are your life.' Compare this with Deuteronomy 30:19–20, where God entreats his people to 'choose life'. Reflect for a moment on what it means to you to have the words of the Bible, and how important it is to heed them.

4

Lions, bulls, dogs and a worm

Read: Psalm 22

I am a worm and not a man... Many bulls surround me (vv. 6, 12).

Consider

There is a well-known game called 'If you were an animal, what would you be?' Sometimes it's played in conversation over dinner or as a parlour game; at other times, it is a left-field interview question. (The safe answer in an interview is reckoned to be 'a dog'—it makes you sound lovable—and the wrong answer is 'a cheetah', because no one likes one of those.) Mostly it is a light-hearted way to think about your and your companions' personalities.

In Psalm 22, however, the narrator makes animal comparisons in a much more dejected frame of mind. He has decided that he is a 'worm' (v. 6). This well describes how he is feeling, from his liquescent bones and innards (v. 14) and the dust that he lies in (v. 15) to the general impression of being lowly and puny. He sees his antagonists as beasts of various kinds—bulls of Bashan (v. 12), lions in the act of attack (v. 13) and some distinctly *un*lovable dogs (v. 16).

This psalm encapsulates a moment. It shows how the psalmist felt as he was writing it, at that particular time. It shows the anatomy of faith under pressure, as a reminder that the world can look like this. Jesus echoed the psalm's opening words on the cross, when he himself was enduring unbelievable suffering. The hope that lingers in the background here is that this is only one day's journal entry. The person who embraces these sentiments may feel like a worm today, but tomorrow, or in three days' time, they may feel very different.

Write

Adapt the animal game slightly to make a journal entry. Consider whether you have been feeling weak or strong, smart or dishevelled, keen or lazy. What animal would best describe your recent sense of self? Have you been different creatures in different places and circumstances? Have the people around you been wild or domesticated, approachable or unpredictable?

You could write a simple journal entry in which you note the animals that you came up with, and why, or you could write something more creative in the manner of Psalm 22, where you describe what the metaphorical animals are doing and tell God how you feel about it.

Share

In a group, decide what sort of animal you and the other group members are. Agree beforehand that this is a bit of fun and no one should feel insulted! Share your answers and compare each individual's perception of themselves with how the group perceives them. This is a good exercise for getting to know each other.

When you have completed your journalling based on Psalm 22, discuss some of the different 'animals' that you have come across at work, at church, in clubs and activities, in positions of responsibility and in passing encounters. Do it with the intention of praying for some of these people: this should prevent your conversation from descending into gossip or outright contempt.

Go further

- Spend some time reflecting on other animal comparisons in the Bible, such as Matthew 10:16 ('I am sending you out like sheep among wolves. Therefore be as shrewd as snakes and as innocent as doves'), and Revelation 13, which mentions a dragon, a leopard, a bear, a lion and a lamb. Why do books of the Bible use animal comparisons like this? What effect does it have or the reader or listener?
- The 'peaceable kingdom' passage in Isaiah 11:6–9 looks forward to animals and humans living in good-natured accord. Search online for art and music with the title 'peaceable kingdom'.
- Make a note to revisit your journal entry in a few days' time. When you do, ask yourself whether you still feel the same as when you wrote it.

A note on the passage

'Bulls of Bashan' (v. 12) were renowned for their quality, since the region was fertile and a centre for agriculture. In Amos 4:1 there is a corresponding reference to 'cows of

Bashan' as a metaphor for women who are impressive and overbearing. But it is not enough to be strong; it is important to be compassionate as well. So when we are talking about people, being numbered among Bashan's bovines is hardly a compliment!

5

Samson's riddle

Read: Judges 14

'Out of the eater, something to eat; out of the strong, something sweet' (v. 14)

Consider

People like a riddle to solve. Many newspapers devote a page to cryptic crosswords, dingbats and the like. They are mostly abstract puzzles, providing a distraction from, rather than a connection with, real life. On the other hand, the reason we relish a leisurely conundrum may be that it warms us up for a genuine test, whenever it may come. After all, we face riddles and dilemmas nearly every day in our work and our relationships, and somehow they need to be solved.

Rather than being an abstract puzzle, Samson's riddle in Judges 14 is concocted from two personal experiences—a divine gift of strength that allowed him to kill a lion (v. 6) and a providential discovery of honey in the lion's carcass (v. 8). These are both extraordinary incidents, and perhaps Samson is still trying to make sense of who he is and how God has provided for him when he comes up with his riddle. The essence of a riddle is a seeming contradiction, so finding something good and sweet in the middle of something ferocious gives him perfect riddling material.

Of course, the riddle is not just for Samson's own benefit. On the occasion of his marriage feast, he wants to set a public challenge. 'Tell us your riddle. Let's hear it,' call out his companions, encouraging him (v. 13). The clue is too cryptic, though; try as they might, they cannot make any sense of it. This is a curious feature of riddles, that they both disclose and withhold information. Rather than working patiently at the puzzle, Samson's rivals extract the solution by force (v. 15).

Write

Think of a paradox or contradiction you have experienced— for instance, a situation where something pleasing was found in the middle of something threatening (or vice versa). Write down what baffled you or what made a solution difficult. For a creative approach, journal these experiences in the form of a riddle, making it as brief as verse 14 or using a longer poetic form.

Verse 4 of the passage indicates that God is working in the background of Samson's feats and fiascos. Can you see how God may be at work in the situation you have journalled?

Share

Riddle writing is a particularly good exercise for sharing with a group (assuming that they are more sympathetic than Samson's audience!). Take it in turns to read your riddles or perhaps lay them out on a table for everyone to examine. Spend some time guessing what each one refers to; see how close you can get. Then ask everyone to reveal the solutions, and talk about how you all dealt with the situations they describe.

Go further

- When you are faced with a dilemma, do you work patiently through it or are you inclined to force a solution?
- Working with riddles is a recurring theme in scripture. The parables Jesus told were, in effect, extended riddles. Read Matthew 13 and notice how Jesus' stories partly revealed and partly concealed truth. Why did Jesus choose to do this?

A note on the passage

The morality of Samson's life in Judges 13—16 takes some untangling. He is headstrong and compulsive, violent and lustful. He is larger than life, and often goes beyond the pale. God works through his actions (Judges 14:4), but then God also worked through the actions of Judas Iscariot. Why should we have any sympathy for Samson?

There is a thread of faithfulness that runs through Samson's sometimes unruly behaviour. The flipside of being headstrong is being determined. Samson was a powerhouse at a weak moment in Israel's history, so, while some of that power is misdirected, Samson's final act in Judges 16 is exemplary. Weak but suddenly strong, he turns out to be the sort of person who would surrender his own life to deliver his fellows from their oppressors. The Bible has a lot of time for people like this.

6
The decisive moment

Read: Ruth 1:6–17; 2:1–12; 4:2–6

As it turned out, she found herself working in a field belonging to Boaz (2:3).

Consider

The Decisive Moment is the title of a classic photographic book by Henri Cartier-Bresson, a pioneer of photojournalism. The phrase also describes his philosophy of photography: knowing when to press the shutter release depends on noticing, in a split second, the moment when history takes a certain course. Decisive moments are often fleeting but, if we can freeze them on film, then we can dwell on their significance. This is perhaps one reason why, in an age of video, photography still remains popular.

Capturing turning points in writing is a more leisurely activity than snapping photographs, but it is essentially the same task. The book of Ruth is a well-told story and contains a number of decisive moments. In chapter 1, there is the fork in the road where Ruth elects to stay with her mother-in-law and live with the religion of Judah. In chapter 2, by good chance, Ruth finds herself working in the field of Boaz, the man who will make all the difference to her future. In chapter 4, there is the outcome of the open-air court case that clears the way for Ruth and Boaz to marry. In the last five verses of the book, it is revealed that these events constitute a large-scale decisive moment in Israel's history, as Ruth bears a child in the future royal line of David.

Write

Give some thought to the decisive moments you have experienced, whether they are recent, small-scale events or key episodes that have determined the path of your life (or the life of your church or community). Spend some time writing about them in your journal. How do these turning points still affect you today? With the benefit of hindsight, can you see God's wider purposes in the way things have turned out? Look at the events in freeze-frames, so as to understand them better. If you like, aim to document events in a reportage style, narrating stand-out details and their significance.

Note that in chapter 1, Ruth's decision to stay with Naomi (v. 16) was about continuing with her direction of travel rather than changing course. This might characterise some of the things you choose to journal: resolving to press on can be as pivotal as a complete change of circumstances.

Share

A good way to introduce this topic in a journalling group is for each member to bring a photo with them that depicts an important time in their life. Begin the meeting by discussing what was happening in each person's photo. (This is another good opportunity to understand your fellow group members more fully.)

Since today's material deals with a whole book of the

Bible, it may be worth reminding yourself of the story before you read the individual passages. If people have reasonable Bible knowledge, try to piece together the story as a group without looking. Alternatively, you could find a summary of the book of Ruth and read it out.

If the group is going to try journalling decisive moments in a reportage style, it might be helpful to find some newspaper articles that demonstrate the genre. Look for pieces that are written by a special reporter (who is often in a war zone or other startling surroundings), which describe what that person witnessed and the overall impressions they were left with.

Go further

- Have a look at some photojournalism and street photography on the internet (the World Press Photo website is a good place to start: www.worldpressphoto.org).
- Become a reporter yourself: find an event to attend and write up in your church or local community. It might be an organised event or simply a walk around a place that you don't usually visit. (You could put the results in a blog or local magazine, and website editors may be interested in what you're doing.)
- Bring to mind critical events that appear to be on the horizon, whether locally or nationally, and pray about them.

7

Understanding envy

Read: 1 Samuel 18:5–11

'They have credited David with tens of thousands,' [Saul] thought, 'but me with only thousands. What more can he get but the kingdom?' (v. 8)

Consider

Saul's jealousy of David is both easy and difficult to grasp. We easily understand the part of him that is like a child in the playground. The people (the women, in fact) have a chant insinuating that David is better than him, and Saul doesn't like it. Yet at the same time, the words that Saul chooses to hear as a taunt still credit him with success; and ultimately David is an asset to his king and country, something that Saul himself has recognised (v. 5). Why bear David a grudge?

In his classical work *Rhetoric*, there is a section where Aristotle addresses the causes of human emotions. He has this to say about envy:

We feel envy if we fall but a little short of having everything; which is why people in high place and prosperity feel it—they think everyone else is taking what belongs to themselves...

We also envy those whose possession of or success in a thing is a reproach to us: these are our neighbours and equals; for it is clear

that it is our own fault we have missed the good thing in question;
this annoys us, and excites envy in us.[6]

These sorts of insights explain some of Saul's behaviour. He does indeed seem to worry that David is acquiring something that ought to be his (hence his panic-stricken thought, 'What more can he get but the kingdom?'), and David's success has indeed become a reproach to Saul.

Rather than rationalising his envy, Saul succumbs to rage and revenge. David, by complete contrast, clings resolutely to his principles and refuses to make his king his rival. This becomes clear in 1 Samuel 24, where David has the opportunity to kill Saul but desists because of his respect for 'the Lord's anointed'.

Write

Who are the people you are naturally tempted to envy? Make a list of people in your journal and write what it is about them or their success that you feel should be yours. Give it some thought: get to the bottom of what is going on inside you, trying to understand these 'Saul' instincts.

Once you have done this, journal your more noble 'David' principles, those that you can honour to keep yourself from unrestrained envy. How does God view you and the people on your list? What would be unreasonable or exaggerated in your mind if you were to envy them? What better way than jealousy can you envisage? Ask God to help you maintain your worthier attitudes. You could even compose a prayer that you can turn to in envious moments.

Share

In a group, discuss the quotation from Aristotle above. Is this a fair assessment of what breeds envy, or are there other causes? Can jealousy have a positive effect if it makes us aim for higher things? (Aristotle believed so.) You could discuss these ideas in general before spending some time journalling individually.

Go further

- The song in verse 7 was popular with many people but, at the same time, aggravated one particular person. Can you think of examples of words, lyrics, films or programmes that delight some people while at the same time angering others? What is a Christian approach to these situations?

A note on the passage

Saul's jealousy seems all the more irrational when you bear in mind that to credit one person with thousands of conquests and another with tens of thousands was simply a convention in Hebrew poetry. It didn't imply that the second person was worthy of greater honour than the first, but, in his paranoia, Saul finds insecurity everywhere. Perhaps he is also affronted that David is mentioned in the same breath as himself, the king. This would reinforce Aristotle's idea that people in high places are bothered if others seem to take any part of the homage they believe is rightfully theirs.

8

Going into detail

Read: 2 Chronicles 3:1–7

*He panelled the main hall with juniper and covered it with
fine gold and decorated it with palm tree and chain designs. He
adorned the temple with precious stones. And the gold he used
was gold of Parvaim (vv. 5–6).*

Consider

Why is the Chronicler so painstaking in his description of
Solomon's temple? One straightforward answer is that he
was doing his job. In keeping an account of Israel's growth
as a nation, his attention to detail is a mark of being consci-
entious. However, in passages such as 2 Chronicles 3, it is
possible to detect something beyond mere accuracy. There is
a certain relish in the particulars. There is a fascination with
the finery, a desire to demonstrate how impressive it all was,
so that even the provenance of the gold is recorded (v. 6).
At first glance, this might look like unfettered materialism.
Read on, though, and these catalogues and inventories are
part of a gathering glory. The concern of the Chronicler is
for everything the temple stands for. By 5:13, the building is
filled not only with praise but with the presence of God.

When people are really interested in something, they often
go into detail about it. Sometimes they overdo it but their

zeal is still endearing. Think of the way railway enthusiasts can reel off the vital statistics of a steam engine, or the way gardeners can tell you the Latin names, preferred soil types and propagation techniques for the plants in their care. Beneath such knowledge lies deep appreciation.

Going into detail avoids becoming idolatry if, at its heart, it is a form of praise. Finely wrought things are possible, and they can be turned to the glory of God. This is what chroniclers past and present have always known.

Write

Think of something that you would happily go into detail about. It could be anything—a miracle of construction, a musical instrument, a prized possession, or a treat for the senses. Sit near the object if this is possible (or look at a picture of it), and write down everything about it that fascinates you. Revel in the detail and have fun choosing your words.

Reflect a little on how the object of your attention fits in with your faith. Perhaps, like a church building, it has a specific spiritual purpose. Perhaps, like a flower of the field, it is simply something that fills you with wonder and praise.

Share

People find all sorts of things fascinating in a way that others find difficult to understand. Begin a journalling group meeting by taking it in turns to answer the question, 'What objects do you find really interesting?', trying to communicate what it is that really captivates you.

You can then spend some journalling time going into

detail. Alternatively, you could agree to write individually beforehand and read out your descriptions when you meet up. If you live near an inspiring public building, you could arrange to have your meeting there (coffee shops are good places to convene).

When you have finished journalling, discuss how you found the exercise. Are you wary of this sort of materialism? Do some objects seem more worthy of attention than others? Have you learned a new appreciation of something by hearing another person's passion?

Go further

- Remind yourself of places of worship that you have visited where the design or adornment has led you to worship.
- In his book *View from a Bouncy Castle*, Adrian Plass recounts a chance experience of watching a couple at a train station who were delighted by a simple table they had bought. Plass found himself moved by 'the depth of pure appreciation I had just seen', and made a link with Paul's exhortation in Philippians 4:8 that we should dwell on whatever is pure, lovely and admirable.[7]

9

The naked hero

Read: Job 1

In the land of Uz there lived a man whose name was Job.
This man was blameless and upright; he feared God and
shunned evil (v. 1).

Consider

People need to be inspired by other people. Stories have
long been told about heroes, saints and shining examples,
about the feats they achieved and the ordeals they withstood.
Heracles the demigod possessed the strength to hold up
the sky; Admiral Nelson had the nous to conquer the sea;
Captain Oates did not shrink from his final walk in the snow.

But heroes are no use if their feet don't touch the ground.
Demigods, admirals and Antarctic explorers—if that is all they
are—are too far removed from ordinary life for ordinary people
to relate to them. Champions only become interesting when
their weaknesses are revealed. Achilles (another demigod)
had a vulnerable heel. David Livingstone was considered
incapable by his fellow explorers and died of tropical disease.
Joan of Arc had no education, and courtiers suspected that
she was delusional. Beethoven went deaf and suffered from
depression. It is only when such obstacles come into view that
a person's accomplishments can be seen in perspective.

In the opening chapter of the book that bears his name, Job is introduced as a rather grand exemplar. He is 'the greatest man among all the people of the East' (v. 3), not only because of his family and livestock but because of his legendary righteousness. However, in some heavenly courtroom a challenge is delivered: 'Does Job fear God for nothing?' (v. 9). Every privilege Job has enjoyed is stripped away—his servants, his sheep and oxen, even his children. By the end of the chapter, all Job has is a spirit that is prepared, astonishingly, to carry on worshipping. His robes are in rags as he takes up the refrain, 'Naked I came from my mother's womb, and naked I will depart' (v. 21). In his circumstances and his attitudes he is now a naked hero, a shorn saint; and somehow we are all the more ready to relate to him.

Write

The journalling exercise for Reflection 7 ('Understanding envy') asked you to identify people whose success might provoke jealousy. For this journal entry, identify a different group of people—those who have no special status but have some quality of spirit that is genuinely inspiring. Such people might once have had, as Job did, a position of respect, but have now relinquished it (for instance, someone retired but still active in the community). Or you might think of people who have always been in the background but whose steadfastness has made for worship, fellowship, laughter, a shoulder to cry on or a job always done.

Journal both what you admire about these people and what makes them lowly, so that you have a rounded rather than an unreal picture of them. Finish with a simple, positive summary of their good example, just as Job 1:22 does.

Share

If you are likely to see a person you have journalled about, try to find a moment to tell them what you admire about them. It is genuinely encouraging when people take the trouble to do this.

In a journalling group, spend some time talking about who your heroes were when you were young and who they are now. Are you aware of any flaws in their lives? How much do you mind these weaknesses?

Then do the journalling exercise and describe the people you have written about to the group. Discuss how we should react to the example that such people provide. Should we try to imitate them or simply give thanks that we know them? (*Celtic Daily Prayer*'s introduction to saints' days is useful: 'The life of a saint is not the life of a great man or woman, but of God's life in an ordinary man or woman.'[8])

Go further

- Look for lowly heroism elsewhere in the Bible. Consider the ordeals of Simon Peter, Joseph and, notably, Jesus, the suffering servant.
- Read an obituary column. A well-written obituary will not be coy about the shortcomings in a person's life but neither will it lose sight of what there is to celebrate.
- Philip Yancey's book *Soul Survivor* contains balanced biographies of inspiring characters, including Martin Luther King, Henri Nouwen and John Donne.

10

Hymns private and public

Read: Psalm 42

*As the deer pants for streams of water, so my soul pants
for you, O God (v. 1).*

Consider

Famous journals are, by definition, at once private and public
writings. They are usually personal records, kept close to the
writer while they were being created, but they also turn out
to have value as public documents. The diarist Samuel Pepys
wrote chiefly for himself and recorded some quite intimate
details of his satisfactions, indiscretions and tribulations. One
of his later publishers removed a number of entries that he
felt were simply not suitable to be aired in public. None the
less, Pepys had his diaries written in fair copy, bound and pre-
sented to Magdalene College library in Cambridge, together
with his other valuable books. He must have suspected that
they would be of interest to a wider audience.

Psalm 42 has a very personal ring to it. The psalmist is
introspective to the point of addressing his own soul (vv. 5,
11). There is an intimate disclosure of tears (v. 3), of sadness
and solace in the night (vv. 3, 8), and of an inward ache that
reaches to the bone (v. 10). At the same time, this psalm,
along with many others, has been bound and preserved for

the benefit of future readers. It has become one of the most public discourses in the world, an outstanding illustration of what it means to wrestle emotionally with oneself and with God. It is offered as a pattern for praying through our longings.

Write

Many people have found that it can be a valuable exercise to rewrite a psalm (evangelist Oswald Chambers was a devotee of this practice). For your journal entry today, notice the train of thought in Psalm 42 and emulate it, writing your own words of sadness and solace. Make it personal. Take turns in addressing both God and your own soul, as the psalmist does. Where Psalm 42 appeals to the rural imagery of the Middle East (deer, streams, the heights of Hermon, Mount Mizar, waterfalls, and so on), make the similes in your psalm local and up to date. (For example, if you work in a city, your psalm might begin, 'As evening commuters long for home, so longs my soul for you, O God.') When you are finished, you will have created a spiritual and emotional record of this time and place in your life.

Share

Here are a few questions for a group to discuss. (You can use these either before or after you have done your own journalling.)

- When you are emotionally or spiritually weary, what are the places, activities or things that help you regain your strength?

- Who do you imagine speaking the psalm? (The psalmist? An ancient congregation? You?)
- What is the prevailing mood of this psalm? (Hope? Despair? Something else?)

It is an important principle in journalling that you should write first and foremost for yourself (see the Introduction for a discussion on this subject). In your journalling today, think carefully about which parts you will make public and which parts you will keep to yourself, and continue to bear this balance in mind in future. Each group member might choose a single sentence to read aloud, just to give a glimpse of ideas that are otherwise personal.

Go further

- Do you share your thoughts and feelings with others enough? Do you sometimes go too far? Ask God to help you get the balance right.
- Issues of privacy and the press are contentious in today's world. Look through a newspaper or news summary. Ask yourself whether all the reports you are reading ought to be in the public domain, and whether as a society we have got the right balance between making things known and leaving them alone. At the same time, give thanks for psalmists, diarists, columnists and all those who are courageous enough to share their innermost thoughts with other people.

A note on the passage

Attempts have been made to identify the geographical location described in verses 6–7. It is possible, for example, that the psalmist is thinking of particular adjacent waterfalls where 'deep calls to deep'. By and large, though, this is to miss the point. Psalm 42 is primarily an expressive piece of writing, and the inward emotions represented by the sounds and images in verse 7 cannot be easily dissected and analysed. It is, however, a fine example for anyone undertaking some searching spiritual journalling.

11

The distillation of wisdom

Read: Proverbs 17:1–10

The crucible for silver and the furnace for gold, but the Lord tests the heart' (v. 3).

Consider

Every culture has its proverbs. They are a way of distilling wisdom—taking the lessons that a person has learned in his or her life and condensing them into a short, pithy form of words so that the wisdom can be passed on.

By themselves, however, proverbs are just snappy sayings that easily become meaningless in the mind and mouth of someone who isn't really thinking. This is illustrated in Cervantes' *Don Quixote*, a tale that is full of wise-sounding sayings coming from foolish lips. In particular, Don Quixote's unlettered companion Sancho is fond of quoting proverbs in an attempt at gentility, but his use of them is indiscriminate.

'The fact is,' continued Sancho, 'that, as your worship knows better than I do, we are all of us liable to death, and today we are, and tomorrow we are not, and the lamb goes as soon as the sheep, and nobody can promise himself more hours of life in this world than God may be pleased to give him; for death is deaf, and when it comes to knock at our life's door, it is always urgent,

and neither prayers, nor struggles, nor sceptres, nor mitres, can
keep it back, as common talk and report say, and as they tell us
from the pulpits every day.'

    'All that is very true,' said Don Quixote; 'but I cannot make
out what thou art driving at.'⁹

We have to approach proverbs more thoughtfully than this
if we are to find any real value in them. Otherwise we will
become lost in their volume and variety in a similar way
to Sancho. The Bible's book of Proverbs contains many
morsels but they should be savoured, not scoffed. Better to
spend time digesting them thoroughly than to regurgitate
fragments endlessly. Better to use proverbs to nurture godly
wisdom than to worship the words themselves. Better to read
proverbs until we are ready to write our own than never to
stop reading them.

Write

Read the sample of sayings in Proverbs 17 until you have a
feel for their language and structure. Note how some proverbs
are simple observations about life (vv. 1–2), while others
have a religious dimension (vv. 3, 5). Some are positive and
optimistic (v. 6); others are stern and political (v. 9). Note
also the many different kinds of people involved—servants,
parents, children, friends and fools.

    Bring to mind some of the lessons that you have learned
about how life works. As in the Bible passage, they might be
in a variety of areas—family life, politics or society in general.
Then journal some insights in the form of proverbs. Work
out what principles are in play when life situations seem to
repeat themselves, and distil your observations into concise

sentences. See if you can include some proverbs that bring God into the picture.

Share

Begin a journalling group meeting by thinking of as many proverbs as you can (whether or not from the Bible) in the space of a minute. Discuss what you think is the point of proverbs.

As you look at the Bible passage, discuss the proverbs one by one. Do you understand each verse? Do you agree with them or is there an alternative point of view? Can you relate any of these proverbs to a real-life situation?

When you have written some proverbs, read them out to each other.

Go further

- There is a mention in Luke's Gospel of Jesus cultivating wisdom (2:47, 52). Reflect on the place of wisdom in the Bible and in Christian living.
- Find some vivid and bizarre proverbs from around the world (for instance, the Ethiopian proverb 'Do not blame God for creating the tiger; be thankful he didn't give him wings.')

12

Less is blessed

Read: Ecclesiastes 12:9–14

The Teacher searched to find just the right words, and what he wrote was upright and true (v. 10).

Consider

Yesterday's material discussed the importance of reading words of wisdom with care rather than in quantity. The conclusion to Ecclesiastes explains that this is also how such words have been written. The 'Teacher' has distilled what he had to say to a minimum as he 'searched to find just the right words' (v. 10). He has done so because verbal excess is a writer's ill discipline and a reader's burden; hence the remark, 'Of making many books there is no end, and much study wearies the body' (v. 12).

All of these observations are made in a composed 'evening mood'. Following a meditation on the evening of life (vv. 1–8), the author is ready to end. Now is not the time for a detailed hearing; rather, now is the time for the summing up. 'All has been heard,' runs the epilogue; 'here is the conclusion of the matter' (v. 13). After all the philosophising and soul-searching of Ecclesiastes, the final word is startlingly simple: 'Fear God and keep his commandments.'

There is a time for this kind of simplicity in our own daily routines. If there are difficulties in the daytime, there should also be easiness in the evening. The New Zealand Prayer Book's order for Night Prayer includes these succinct and settling words:

Lord, it is night.
The night is for stillness.
Let us be still in the presence of God.

It is night after a long day.
What has been done has been done;
what has not been done
has not been done; let it be.

Write

In your journalling today, make simplicity a hallmark as you 'search to find just the right words' to describe the point you have reached. Here are some different approaches you can try:

- Sum up your day in just three words (for example, 'Hard but rewarding' or 'Who's in charge?')
- If you have been busy with many different things, choose a single matter that is worth writing about and concentrate on it.
- If you are writing in the evening, write an epilogue for the day. This can be in poetry or prose (both appear in the passage from Ecclesiastes). It should be pithy, and should conclude the day's business rather than complicating it.

Share

Begin a journalling group meeting by taking turns to sum up your day in three words. Allow some time to explain these summaries and catch up with each other. Make your meeting conducive to an 'evening mood': serve drinks or share food, sit outside in warm weather, sit around a fire in cold weather, use comfortable seats, dim the lights.

After looking at Ecclesiastes and doing some journalling, you could finish with a form of night prayer (or other prayers suitable for the time of day).

If your simple journalling has produced a creative gem or two, consider whether it might find a place in a local publication, a blog or a social networking post.

Go further

- Look for other parts of the Bible that seem to be written in a becalmed frame of mind. Psalm 131 is a good example.
- Having described the day in three words, go a step further and write a haiku poem. Find examples of haiku (which generally have lines of five, then seven, then five syllables). Write your own haiku to summarise something you have been thinking about.

A note on the passage

The need to respect concise and authoritative words of wisdom is underlined in verse 12: 'Be warned, my son, of anything in addition to them.' Amendments might dilute or change the original message. Similar warnings are made elsewhere in the Bible. Deuteronomy 4:2 says that the Lord's commands are to be preserved without addition or subtraction, and in Revelation 22:18–19 (another epilogue) there are repercussions for would-be editors or embellishers of the text.

13

A love that learns to speak its name

Read: Song of Songs 7

Let us go early to the vineyards to see if the vines have budded…
there I will give you my love (v. 12).

Consider

You may have heard the phrase 'the love that dare not speak its name'. It comes from a poem by Lord Alfred Douglas, the lover of Oscar Wilde, and gave rise to a line of questioning during Wilde's trial. In a sense, the poem itself was put in the dock as Wilde was asked, 'What is "the love that dare not speak its name"?' Wilde maintained that it referred to a noble and classical form of love, but the phrase (and indeed the trial) has become associated with a relationship that was furtive, frowned upon, publicised, sensationalised and ultimately condemned. The context of Victorian homosexuality laws may be unfamiliar now but the wider issue is still familiar—that human love can become desperate and tainted by shame and rejection.

In complete contrast, Song of Songs offers a vision of love that is copious and carefree. Its garden setting, with abundant fruitfulness, a profusion of sensual experiences and a celebration of the body, recall the Eden of Genesis 2, where there was no shame in nakedness and where a fluent companionship existed between man, woman and God. Song of Songs is so unfettered that, in the past, people have preferred to interpret the book as an allegory of the ideal love between God and humankind. There is something in this, but we should not miss the permission that the book seems to give us to delight in the sensual, the visceral and the physical. 'May the wine go straight to my beloved, flowing gently over lips and teeth' (v. 9) is one enchanting example. Ultimately the poetry hopes for a fulfilment of love that is completely good and satisfying: this is what the imagery of verse 12 is all about.

Write

Use your journal as an opportunity to be candid with yourself. What is your situation with love at the moment? What different types of relationship are there in your life, and what do you hope for? Be judicious in your thinking and bear in mind the caution in Song of Songs that love should not be awakened at the wrong time and place (2:7; 3:5; 8:4), but recognise also what you can desire and delight in without shame. See if you can assign images, scents and sensations to your relationships and write them down in poetry or prose. Love is all-important for human beings; take some steps towards naming freely how and who you love.

Share

This journal entry is probably one to keep to yourself rather than sharing with a group. However, you can discuss how easy or difficult you found it to write. Do you prefer to keep thoughts about love private or do you like to wear your heart on your sleeve? Are we reluctant to reveal ourselves because we live in a world that likes a scandal, or is guarding our feelings simply being human?

Go further

- Find out about the different types of love that C.S. Lewis discusses in his book *The Four Loves*. Notice the relative importance he attaches to each type, and the way they depend on each other.

A note on the passage

The commentator Barry Webb writes, 'The Song of Songs is there to stop love going out of our relationships, with God and with one another. It is a splendid garment, to be worn not with awkwardness or embarrassment, but festively, with joy and deep thankfulness to Him who gave it to us as Holy Scripture.'[10]

14

What does the Lord say?

Read: Isaiah 43

*'See, I am doing a new thing! Now it springs up; do you not
perceive it?' (v. 19).*

Consider

Stephen Covey's bestselling book *The 7 Habits of Highly Effective People* is a call for people to build healthy, deep-rooted
character traits in business and in relationships. Habit five,
'Seek first to understand, then to be understood', questions
whether we really listen to other people properly and recommends that we develop the ability to do so.

> *Communications experts estimate... that only 10 percent of our
> communication is represented by the words we say. Another 30
> percent is represented by our sounds, and 60 percent by our body
> language. In empathic listening, you listen with your ears, but
> you also, and more importantly, listen with your eyes and with
> your heart.*[11]

Christians have often debated how best to hear what God has
to say. (A general conclusion must surely be that no means
should be ruled out if we are talking about a God who is
always capable of surprising us.) Whatever the method, we
can agree that it is important to listen well to God, to become

intently attentive. At the heart of Bible study, *lectio divina*, charismatic gifts, retreat, prayerful mediation, watching the world or any other type of spiritual listening is a straightforward purpose: to understand the heart and purposes of God better.

Passages such as Isaiah 43 encourage us to sharpen our spiritual senses. 'This is what the Lord says,' goes the refrain in verses 1, 14 and 16, and the expectation is that God's people will listen. God also wants them to watch. 'See, I am doing a new thing!' he announces (v. 19). 'Do you not perceive it?' God is speaking, showing, opening his heart.

Although there are words of rebuke in this passage (vv. 22–24), there are also many promises of protection, acceptance and forgiveness (vv. 2, 4, 25). The question is, will the people listen well or will their eyes remain closed and their ears stopped (v. 8)?

Write

Think about these questions on how you tune in to God, and journal your answers.

- What methods of watching and listening to God do you use? Are there others you might give time to?
- When you give God your attention, are you trying to understand his overarching plans (as in much of Isaiah 43) or his specific daily guidance? Should you be doing more of one or the other?
- Are you prepared to hear both encouragement and criticism when you listen to God?
- What in particular might God have in store for you, your family, your friends or your church? Even if you

are not sure of the answer, half of the point is to seek to understand God's purposes earnestly and prayerfully.

Share

In a journalling group, begin by thinking of the things that most demand your careful attention. You might include an important part of your work, such as professional listening skills, or something recreational, like playing an instrument.

Discuss the questions above together before journalling individually. You may find it interesting to hear how other people listen to God and how they believe they have heard him. When it comes to the final question about what God has for you, concentrate on the areas you share as a group. What might God want to say to your neighbourhood, for instance, or your church?

Go further

- The anthropologist Tanya Luhrmann has spent time in a number of charismatic churches, trying to understand how church members listen for God's guidance. Her write-ups have been received with interest by both church members and outsiders. You can read articles about her research online.[12]
- The idea that ears, eyes and hearts may be either open or closed is introduced early in Isaiah, in 6:9–10. Look at the way this passage is used in the New Testament to make a point about believing in Jesus (or not): see John 12:37–42 and Acts 28:23–28.

A note on the passage

In verse 15, God is called 'Israel's Creator'. There is an emphasis on this name in Isaiah 40—55, where God is called 'Creator' or 'Maker' more times than anywhere else in the Old Testament. Partly, this is to remind people that they owe God their existence, but it is also a reminder of the idea we explored in Reflection 1, that God is always able to make new things happen.

15

The lyrics of injustice

Read: Isaiah 59

*So justice is driven back, and righteousness stands at a distance;
truth has stumbled in the streets, honesty cannot enter (v. 14).*

Consider

Protest songs are a clever idea. Protest is aggressive and often hard to hear. Songs, on the other hand, are appealing and infectious. People who put their message to music balance prickly words with a good tune, so that the listener wants to keep listening. A good example is Sam Cooke's 'A change is gonna come', an anthem of the American Civil Rights movement. The song is about inequality and suffering, but the melody is languid and soulful. This fashioning of protest, making it more than mere shouting, can also be achieved without music. Martin Luther King, for instance, delivered speeches with a distinctively lyrical quality.

The book of Isaiah says a great deal about injustice, yet the message is curiously and continuously lyrical. 'Righteousness stands at a distance', says 59:14; 'truth has stumbled in the streets.' The words almost make you want to look out of the window and see. This portrayal of wrong is affecting without being hectoring. Even if you're appalled, you want to keep listening to such lyrics because the message is delivered so well.

Write

Identify a situation that strikes you as particularly unjust and write down how you feel about it. Do this creatively in the form of a speech, a poem or even a protest song if you like. Temper the frustrating facts with lyrical flair in the manner of Isaiah 59. Lay bare the stains, the violence, the crookedness, the darkening, the growling and the moaning (as in verses 3–11). Paint a vivid picture and appeal to the heart.

Share

See if you can share, sensitively, what you have written—whether with one or two people or as an online post—so that, whatever your concern is, you have started to talk about it (always the first step in confronting injustice). If you are part of a writing group, read your journalling aloud and then spend some time discussing the issues that have been raised.

One commentator has this to say about Isaiah 59:15b–16: 'The great hope of the world is that God sees! He is neither blind nor insensitive. He sees and hears the clamour of the Sodoms of this world and decrees that their sin will have a limit.'[13] Discuss how far Christians should take action, and how far we should look to God to prevent injustice.

Go further

- Review your own dealings with issues of injustice. How do you hear about injustice? How do you choose what to concentrate on and pray for? How do you pass on disturbing news? What action can you take?

- Listen to some protest songs written from a Christian perspective. 'If we are the body' by Casting Crowns and 'The trouble with normal' by Bruce Cockburn are a couple to start with. 'Sing me a song with social significance' from the musical *Pins and Needles* is an adept apology for the protest song.
- Struggles for justice (often based on real life) make ready material for movies. *Erin Brockovich* is a study of underdogs taking a stand against corporate exploitation. *The Rum Diary* (based on Hunter S. Thompson's book) tells the story of a journalist, caught up in a world of corruption and greed, gradually finding his voice. Towards the end he sits alone and types, 'I will try and speak for my reader. That is my promise. And it will be a voice made of ink and rage.'

A note on the passage

Verse 17, in which God puts on a breastplate of righteousness and a helmet of salvation, has a parallel in Ephesians 6:14–17. The difference is that, whereas in the Old Testament there is no one but God to fight the good fight, in the New Testament a whole church of believers is called to arms.

16

Interpreting the occasion

Read: Psalm 45

*My heart is stirred by a noble theme as I recite my verses
for the king (v. 1).*

Consider

Where there's pomp there's a poem. During Britain's summer
of 2012, for instance, Carol Ann Duffy produced *Jubilee Lines*,
a collection of 60 poems to celebrate the Queen's 60-year
reign. The Olympic Games were accompanied by an entire
Cultural Olympiad, including the 'Poetry Parnassus' event
in London. Lyricists are important interpreters of the times;
they are the people who remind us what it all means.

It was always thus. Psalm 45 was written, we are told in
the introductory note, as a royal wedding song. This early
poet laureate extols the king, 'the most excellent of men' (v.
2), and the beauty of the bride (v. 11). From the beginning,
the tone rises to the occasion: 'My heart is stirred by a noble
theme'. But the psalmist is no sycophant, and these verses
do not just honour the king, they remind him of the values
that uphold the kingdom. The throne that will last for ever is
first of all God's (v. 6), and victory must be pursued only in a
just cause (v. 4).

Psalm 45 is a good example of how celebrity status and a sense of occasion can be kept in healthy balance by remembering a higher power and a greater majesty. The psalmist, in fact, celebrates two kings—the one who is on the throne and the one who sustains the kingdom.

Write

Spend some time journalling about an important occasion, either national or personal. Meditate on this milestone and write about its significance to make sense of it. Reflect on the spiritual meaning of the event; keep in mind not just the personalities and any glamour involved, but also the one to whom everyone is ultimately answerable.

Share

You could, like the psalmist, write for someone else's special occasion. A piece of writing can make a very personal gift. It can also be unusual: how much thought do people typically give to the remarks written in cards for birthdays or even weddings? There may be an occasion around the corner for which your carefully chosen words would make a good present. It may even be appropriate to spell out the spiritual significance of the event—for instance, at a baptism.

If you are journalling in a group, take your pick from the two exercises above. You could write about an occasion close to your own heart, explain the event to the group and then share your journal. Alternatively, work in pairs, telling each other as much as you can about a forthcoming occasion and then writing some lines for the other person's benefit.

Since Psalm 45 is a wedding song, you could conclude a

group meeting by voting for your favourite wedding hymn or song.

Go further

- Compare Psalm 45 with your national anthem (use the full version if you are looking at the UK's anthem). Note the similarities. Are these verses timeless or does anything seem out of date?
- Find out about Gary Chapman's book *The 5 Love Languages*. One of the 'languages' that certain people respond to is 'words of appreciation'. Which people around you are particularly encouraged by words? Which are particularly good at encouraging others in this way?

A note on the passage

The advice to the bride in verse 10, 'Forget your people and your father's house', is rather startling. Undoubtedly patriarchy and monarchy are tied up in this verse. Maintaining good order was a priority in an ancient monarchy, and everyone, even the queen, had to know who to answer to (see also verse 11). If this seems overbearing to us today, and not the sort of idea we ourselves would include if we were celebrating an event in verse, perhaps we can still respect the psalmist's overall concern to uphold virtues as well as celebrities.

17

Jeremiah's complaint

Read: Jeremiah 20:7–18

So the word of the Lord has brought me insult and reproach all day long. But if I say, 'I will not mention his word or speak any more in his name,' his word is in my heart like a fire, a fire shut up in my bones (vv. 8b–9).

Consider

In today's world, complaints usually revolve around minor inconveniences. We can cope with our grievances as long as there is some sort of structure. There should be a procedure for complaints; there should be a hotline. It is annoying having to phone up about a problem that wasn't our fault in the first place, but often the call is free and on the other end of the line are people who have to be polite to us. Most things seem to get sorted out in the end.

Jeremiah's complaint, however, is of a completely different kind. His is a hard calling. His prophecies are dreadful and depressing and they have a cumulative effect on the prophet himself. The result is full-blown emotional and spiritual disenchantment: 'Cursed be the day I was born!' (v. 14). Jeremiah's exasperation is the result of being pulled in two directions. On the one hand, 'the word of the Lord has brought... insult and reproach all day long'; on the other, his vocation is so much a part of him that he cannot turn aside from it. His complaint is the venting of pressure. There is no support structure here, no handy customer helpline; it is just Jeremiah and God, the one telling the other how he feels.

Write

Our lives are rarely in perfect balance; most of us are working through at least one difficult situation at any given time. The question is not so much whether we have a complaint but how serious our complaint is and whether we have been talking to God about it. Spend some time mulling over your recent complaints (here defining 'complaint' not as a kind of cynicism but rather as the simple naming of something that you find hard to cope with).

For a journalling exercise, you could spell out the frustrations of a certain situation and note the forces that are pulling you in different directions. You may even have experienced dissatisfaction in the course of your service to God. Like Jeremiah, your thoughts may feel torn, so that one moment you have confidence in God and the next you wish that none of this was your lot. Letting off steam and writing these frustrations down may be helpful in itself.

If you prefer, try something more light-hearted. Write an indignant 'letter to the editor', beginning with something like 'Dear Sir/Madam, I wish to complain in the strongest possible terms...' and continuing with the impossibilities and absurdities of your situation. Many people feel better for writing a letter like this, whether or not it is actually sent.

After you have finished writing, spend some time asking God to help you with whatever pressure points you face.

Share

It is sometimes said (particularly of the British) that we spend plenty of time complaining about people behind their backs but never mention the matter to the people directly involved who could make a difference. If it would be good to have a frank conversation with someone, think about how you could arrange it.

The second of the two journalling exercises above may be the best one to use in a group. It can be quite entertaining to read out your 'letters to the editor' (in a suitably huffy tone). Afterwards, share in more detail about the situations they refer to. What bearing does your faith have on these dilemmas?

Go further

- Compare Jeremiah's complaint with the prophet Jonah's. Rather like Jeremiah, Jonah grumbles, 'It is better for me to die than to live' (Jonah 4:3). The difference is that Jonah is aggrieved not by God's judgement but by his forbearance. For this peculiar prophet, the news is *not bad enough*. (Jonah is the subject of Reflection 19.)
- Some church traditions mark the new year with a Covenant Service, an opportunity for the whole congregation to renew their Christian commitment. Abandonment to God's will and a determination to accept the rough with the smooth are common features of the prayers used in these services (you can find them online by searching for 'covenant service').

18

Sorting sorrow

Read: Lamentations 3:1–33

*I remember my affliction and my wandering, the bitterness and
the gall... Yet this I call to mind and therefore I have hope
(vv. 19, 21).*

Consider

Some of the first things that we give children as toys are
about making order out of a jumble. Shape sorters, building
blocks and jigsaws are a few examples. From these early
days onwards, living in the world requires us to order our
thoughts and draw shapes round our experiences. We learn
to use diaries and timetables; we learn to write reports and
summaries. We even learn to keep journals, in which the very
act of 'writing the day behind us' can help us to assimilate
what has happened. When we announce that something is
'sorted', we mean exactly that: we have brought coherence
out of confusion; we have put things in their place.

The author of Lamentations is surrounded by disinte-
gration, some of it physical. The opening of the book is set
within the derelict city of Jerusalem, devoid of her exiled or
slaughtered inhabitants and with a tumbledown infrastruc-
ture. But there is also emotional disarray. In chapter 3, the
speaker feels 'besieged' and 'surrounded' with 'bitterness

and hardship' (v. 5). The catalogue of woes—scorn, poverty, vagrancy, suffering—continues for 20 verses.

The peculiar thing is that the woes are carefully catalogued. That is to say, Lamentations is very far from being a messy spillage of grief on to the page. Even a brief glance reveals that this is poetry, with themes, sections, images and a journey of thought. Look a little closer, and you see that the book has an symmetrical structure (chapters 1, 2, 4 and 5 have 22 verses each, while the middle chapter has 66). In the Hebrew, the poetry is acrostic: that is, the first letter of each verse is selected so as to progress through the Hebrew alphabet, starting at *Aleph*. If this is woe, it is worked-through woe; if it is suffering, it is sorted suffering. Therefore it is no surprise that, from verse 21, the mood begins to change. The author is settled enough to compose his thoughts and to turn his mind to hope, patience and consolation.

Write

As you journal the day or recent events, pay particular attention to knotty problems (some of which you may not have resolved yet). Work through the issues well enough to be able to summarise them. When you have finished, read back over what you have written and see whether the process of writing has made anything clearer.

You can take this a stage further by writing your own acrostic poem. Choose a single word, such as 'FAITH' or 'SORROW', and write the letters vertically down the page. Then start each line of your poem with these letters. As in Lamentations, aim for a journey of thought.

Share

Begin a journalling group meeting by discussing how far you think heartache should be tamed. Have you seen examples of people expressing too much or too little of their emotions?

Go on to the journalling exercise and, if you feel comfortable, read and discuss what you have written. Talking problems through in the company of others is a kind of 'oral journalling' and can be just as helpful in ordering our thoughts.

Go further

- Look for prayers, songs and poems that respond to grief and adversity in a measured way.
- David Runcorn's book *Choice, Desire and the Will of God* devotes a chapter to the importance of lament, arguing that 'lament is the antidote to despair and silence'.[14]
- Jane Austen's novel *Sense and Sensibility* is the story of two sisters who, as the title suggests, are governed by reasonableness and impulsiveness respectively. Chapters 9—11 give a flavour, in which the characters debate how far the emotions should be controlled.

A note on the passage

The particular Hebrew word for the 'man' who speaks (v. 1) refers to someone who is strong and robust. We can infer that he would not crumble at the slightest provocation; we can also conclude that sorting sorrow is not just for wimps.

19

The freedom of finding you're foolish

Read: Jonah 1—2

'Pick me up and throw me into the sea… I know that it is my fault that this great storm has come upon you' (1:12).

Consider

You must picture me alone in that room… night after night, feeling, whenever my mind lifted even for a second from my work, the steady, unrelenting approach of Him whom I so earnestly desired not to meet. That which I greatly feared had at last come upon me. In the Trinity Term of 1929 I gave in, and admitted that God was God, and knelt and prayed: perhaps, that night, the most dejected and reluctant convert in all England.[15]

This is how C.S. Lewis describes his conversion from atheism in his book *Surprised by Joy*. Perhaps it is odd, even though he was clearly being honest, to hear the well-known author and apologist describe his feelings as 'dejected and reluctant' at this point in his life. But Lewis was not only acknowledging the existence of God; he was also having to admit the wrongness of years lived without or even against him. Even as Lewis gave his life to God, he was confronted by his earlier miscalculations.

The prophet Jonah was just such a fool. In the short book named after him, his stubborn attitudes are revealed as ridiculous. He decides to run away from God (1:3) and even tells the ship's crew that this is what he's doing (v. 10). But how is it possible to run away from the God who, according to Jonah's own understanding, 'made the sea and the dry land' (v. 9)? Jonah is so found out by his own foolishness that he *asks* to be thrown into the sea.

God pours no scorn on people for the time they have spent playing the fool. He simply welcomes them back, as C.S. Lewis eventually realised. The account of his conversion continues, 'I did not then see what is now the most shining and obvious thing; the Divine humility which will accept a convert even on such terms.'

So it is with Jonah. If chapter 1 is an account of Jonah's madness, chapter 2 is a litany of right-mindedness. Having admitted the error of his ways, Jonah makes his peace with God.

Write

Jonah reaches the point where he can be quite candid about his folly: 'I know it is my fault' (1:12). But in the same moment he is candid about his faith: 'I am a Hebrew and I worship the Lord' (v. 9). Journal as honestly as you can about your own mad moments and wrong turns. Mention along the way, as Jonah does, the ways in which you have kept faith amid your foolishness. In bringing these things on to the page and into the open, you might just feel the freedom of finding you're foolish.

Share

To be effective, the journalling exercise above is probably best kept private. If you are part of a group, you might like to think of a minor bungle that you can share. If everyone is willing, you can turn this into a light-hearted 'Fools Anonymous' meeting, where people take it in turn to stand and declare, 'My name is [name], and I'm a fool,' and then admit to having done something daft. Our instinct is to cover over our slip-ups, so this may feel awkward at first, but it can be rather refreshing to find, in the face of our own stupidity, that we are still accepted and that we are all fools one way or another.

If you are part of a church fellowship, reflect on whether congregation members are free to admit their mistakes or whether they have to look as if they're doing well. If it is the latter, ask how straightforward honesty can be given a more prominent place.

Go further

- Read some more of C.S. Lewis's *Surprised by Joy*. The quotations above are from chapter 14, 'Checkmate'.
- Consider figures in public life who have confessed their foolishness. Has it been their downfall or has their honesty been to their credit?

A note on the passage

An ancient understanding of the cosmos is at work in Jonah 2, which conceives of an underworld at the 'roots of the mountains', a place where people have reached a physical and spiritual trough. But we do not have to see the universe this way to be absorbed by the poetry of the murky depths to which Jonah sinks (with seaweed wrapped round his head) before he rises again. C.S. Lewis seems to have visited this place, or somewhere like it.

20

The poetry of suffering

Read: Habakkuk 3:17–19

Yet I will rejoice in the Lord, I will be joyful in God my Saviour (v. 18).

Consider

There is a Monty Python sketch in which a son pays a surprise visit to his family home. His mother is a gentle soul. His father is a gruff Yorkshireman who dresses like a blue-collar worker, but he is a playwright. The son is coiffured, wears a suit and talks posh, but he is a coal miner. A family argument quickly ensues because the father believes his son's choice of career is pretentious, a far cry from his own honest labour. 'He's had a hard day, dear,' explains the mother to the son as she pours the tea. 'His new play opens at the National Theatre tomorrow.'

It is the type of sketch that works by turning stereotypes on their head. The stereotypes themselves are well established: in the real world, coal miners do the hard and necessary work while poets and playwrights indulge themselves in whimsy. The stereotype is worth challenging, though. There are occasions when poetry is essential for the survival of the human spirit, even in unglamorous times of toil and suffering. Wilfred Owen wrote verses in the trenches of World War I.

Elton John caught the mood at Princess Diana's funeral with a freshly written version of 'Candle in the wind'. There is a keenly felt need on such occasions to deal with everything that is dreadful and everything that is mundane and to go beyond them in search of something uplifting. This can only be achieved through some sort of poetry.

There are examples in the Bible. One is the conclusion to the book of Habakkuk, which illustrates how poetry can be a way of assimilating hardship. Habakkuk is honest about what he has seen (the livestock have gone and the harvest is hopeless, v. 17), and about how this makes him feel (see 1:1–4), but he sees just as keenly with the eyes of faith. God remains the source of his energy and exuberance (3:18–19). When life becomes austere or frost-bound, finding words like these allows the soul to stay warm.

Write

Bearing in mind a hardship you face, record your thoughts in the way that Habakkuk does. Express candidly what is wrong and how bad things are, but go on to examine the inward glimmer of faith. You could employ Habakkuk's basic structure, '*Though* the situation is this, *yet* I will do this' (see vv. 17–18). Whatever lyrical style you choose, make use of the tools of poetry to excavate your emotions and unearth faith. (Journalling is, we could say, a type of mining.)

Share

Begin a journalling group meeting by talking about the 'image' that poetry has in society. Is it seen as superfluous? Are writers and poets considered cosseted and fanciful?

Have you come across difficult situations in which poetry or performance seemed entirely necessary?

If you are happy to share what has been journalled, you might like to look at each other's work silently rather than reading it aloud. Place your journals (opened at the right page) or loose leaves on a table so that everyone can walk round and read whatever they like.

Go further

- Look at examples of journals that record suffering. A good example is Anne Frank's *Diary of a Young Girl*. Some passages bear comparison with Habakkuk 3. For instance:

  It's a wonder I haven't abandoned all my ideals, they seem so absurd and impractical. Yet I cling to them because I still believe, in spite of everything, that people are truly good at heart... I feel the suffering of millions. And yet, when I look up at the sky, I somehow feel that everything will change for the better, that this cruelty too shall end, that peace and tranquility will return once more.[16]

- Look for music or art that has emerged from suffering—for instance, Eric Clapton's song 'Tears in heaven', or Picasso's *Guernica*. Consider how works like these help people to bear the pain that gave rise to them.

21

Spirited conversation

Read: Matthew 15:21–28

[Jesus] replied, 'It is not right to take the children's bread and toss it to the dogs.' 'Yes it is, Lord,' she said. 'Even the dogs eat the crumbs that fall from their master's table' (vv. 26–27).

Consider

'Don't answer back.' It sounds like an old-fashioned rule that everyone believed in once, a means of preserving respect for elders and betters. In fact, it may be a myth that anyone has ever completely subscribed to this belief. In the Victorian novel *Tom Brown's Schooldays* by Thomas Hughes, headmaster Dr Arnold is held in dread and awe throughout the school. On the first occasion when Tom and his friend East are sent to see 'the Doctor', they are late back from a school run, covered in mud and fearing harsh treatment. They find him making a toy boat with his children. The book reads, 'All looked so kindly, and homely, and comfortable that the boys took heart in a moment,' and continues with a dialogue that shows the headmaster's sympathy as much as his strictness. He is not, as it turns out, a monster who must not be offended; if anything, he has a soft spot for pupils who speak their mind.

In Matthew 15, a Canaanite woman follows after Jesus and his disciples, distressed about her daughter. At first Jesus says nothing and his disciples want rid of her, but the woman is persistent, crying for help on her knees. 'It is not right to take the children's bread and toss it to the dogs,' says Jesus, implying in picture language that his mission is not to the Gentiles. At this point, the woman could have chosen to be polite and not answer back, but there is too much spirit in her for that, and she takes Jesus on, speaking in the same picture language. Far from being angry, Jesus commends her faith and declares her daughter healed.

Did Jesus behave like this on purpose? Did he keep his distance to test the woman's determination? Did he draw the woman in because he wanted to have an enthusiastic exchange? These questions are worth considering for our own prayer life, because we sometimes conceive of God as a headmaster who requires a continual awed deference. The Canaanite woman gives this image the lie. A spirited conversation, it appears, is not out of place.

Write

There are several factors that can keep us from saying what we would really like to say to our heavenly Father—our upbringing, if we have been taught to be polite; our church culture, if God is always addressed in a solemn manner; or simply the matter in hand, which may be painful or theologically confusing. In your journalling today, try to go beyond such constraints. Write down a few things 'from the gut', honest reactions to situations in your everyday or spiritual life. Have the courage to tell God what you really think or to ask questions that demand a good answer.

If you are using the journalling template (see pages 18–19), make a note of your spirited conversation openers in the

'Things to revisit later' column. Jesus had his reasons for his unhurried response in Matthew 15; God may have reasons to respond to your situation in his own time.

Share

Begin a journalling group meeting with a discussion about the place of reverence, both in your own relationship with God and in the wider church. Does reverence protect from overfamiliarity or does it impede honesty?

When you have completed the journalling exercise, each person should decide whether or not they would like to share what they have written. Those who wish to can read it out. Otherwise, they might try to explain what issues they are handling with care.

Go further

- Look at other passages in the Bible where there is a lively exchange between a person and God—for instance, Abraham pleading for Sodom (Genesis 18:16–33) and Moses explaining his nervousness in Exodus 4:10–17.
- If a stern person was influential in your childhood, imagine what you would say to them now about their attitudes. You could even write out an imagined dialogue between the two of you.

22

Inside and out

Read: Psalm 65

*We are filled with the good things of your house, of your holy
temple… The meadows are covered with flocks and the valleys are
mantled with corn; they shout for joy and sing (vv. 4, 13).*

Consider

Ever since landscape architects such as 'Capability' Brown
began to ply their trade, people have liked the idea of houses
being in harmony with the surrounding countryside and
gardens. Spectacular estates such as Chatsworth, Stowe and
Longleat show how terraces, lakes and topography can draw
the eye, so that even someone inside the house is naturally
inclined to look out of the window at the display of nature.

We often have a similar approach to church buildings.
Village churches are part of the landscape, and harvest
services bring nature indoors in the form of wheatsheaves and
pumpkins, so that the boundary is blurred between the place
of worship and the abundance of the world outside. Even in
modern church buildings, we will often use skies, seascapes
and mountain views as a background to PowerPoint displays.
There is an episode of *The Vicar of Dibley* where a stained-glass
window needs replacing in the church. After fundraising and
deliberating about what images should appear in the new

window, ordinary glass is eventually chosen, which gives a beautiful view of the countryside beyond. Church members agree that they can't do better than a view of God's creation.

Psalm 65 begins inside 'the house' and 'the courts' of God's temple (v. 4). The opening verses are recited as if by an indoor congregation, praising God for his faithfulness and forgiveness. Then it is as if doors and windows are thrown open and the vision of the psalm expands to encompass seas, mountains, sunsets, rain showers, crops and fields. Worship inside the temple mingles with the glory of meadows and valleys, all singing the same glad song (v. 13). It is a wonderful unison of inside and out.

Write

Journal some things you can thank God for. Rather than simply making a perfunctory list, however, allow yourself to be thrilled by the goodness in God's world. Think of a landscape that you find inspiring or, if possible, go outside so that you can touch, smell and feel what the world is doing. Does anything seem to be singing, dancing or overflowing? Break out of your usual journalling space and make a connection with the many outdoor elements that pulsate with praise; when you come back inside, bring some flowers or branches to put in a vase on your desk. Write as if you are talking to God as the psalmist does, telling him what you see and what you appreciate.

Share

Make a journalling group meeting stimulating to the senses. If you cannot meet outdoors, find some harvest artwork to look at while you listen to Psalm 65 being read. (Try *The Wheatfield* by Raoul Dufy, *Brightwell Church and Village* by John Constable, or Claude Monet's paintings of haystacks.)

For this topic, you might consider combining your journalling on one large piece of paper. Place the paper in the middle of the group where everyone can reach it, and contribute to a written collage of praise and thanksgiving. Make copies when you have finished, or display the paper on a wall.

Go further

- As well as displaying visual art, find some music that expresses the joy of the natural world. John Rutter's setting of 'For the beauty of the earth' is one example. You could also look at poems such as 'God's grandeur' by Gerard Manley Hopkins.
- If you have a camera or enjoy sketching, add some illustrations to your journalling.

A note on the passage

In parallel with the movement of the psalm from indoors to outdoors, there is a broadening vision of who may experience the divine blessing. In verse 4, it is those who live near the temple—people from Israel, who are nourished by God. However, in verses 5 and 8, the scope of God's influence extends to the whole earth. This is important for any worshipper to understand: God bestows his goodness far beyond centres of religion. Jesus made a similar point in Matthew 5:45, that God 'causes his sun to rise on the evil and the good, and sends rain on the righteous and the unrighteous'.

23
Marching orders

Read: Mark 6:6b–11

These were his instructions: 'Take nothing for the journey except a staff—no bread, no bag, no money in your belts' (v. 8).

Consider

In Mark 6, Jesus makes a task force of his disciples, giving them instructions to do the sort of things they have seen him doing—preaching, healing, delivering. These are the first stirrings of what would come to be known as the Church, a group of people who model themselves on Christ and trail his message and ministry through a thousand hamlets and market places.

It is an undertaking that requires a great deal of spiritual focus. To this end, Jesus gives the Twelve a set of 'marching orders', a code of discipline. They must have no extraneous concerns, not even about what they should eat or what they should wear. They must bring themselves under a rule as a means of mission.

It is passages such as this that have prompted Christians ever since to search for the spiritual disciplines that suit their situations. This is true as much for people who keep a spiritual journal or a daily time of quiet as it is for those who enter a religious community with a comprehensive rule. Sometimes there are attempts to develop disciplines on a large scale. The 1974 Lausanne Covenant, for instance, is an internationally recognised schema for mission in our own time. It is interesting that, as in Mark 6, this covenant sees a need for purposeful parsimony: 'Those of us who live in affluent circumstances accept our duty to develop a simple lifestyle in order to contribute more generously to both relief and evangelism.'[17]

Write

Spend some time thinking about the patterns that you currently maintain for your own spiritual resilience. Reading the Bible, attending church meetings, praying at set times, examining your behaviour—in fact, anything that constitutes a positive habit—is worth noting in your journal (and there may be more to note down than you thought). Then make a list of trends in today's culture (for instance, consumerism) that might need to be resisted by developing a rule for living. Is there anything you need to cut back on, bring under control or give up altogether? Write down some 'marching orders' that apply to your own context, which reflect how you think God would like you to live.

Share

After thinking through these things, it might be good to share your conclusions with someone you trust, such as a prayer partner or a trusted church member. If you want to try following a particular discipline, mention this as well: you will probably take it more seriously if someone else knows about it.

In a journalling group, you could start with a discussion about monasteries, convents and people in religious orders. What do you admire in these communities and what do you find offputting?

You could then either use the individual exercise above or all contribute to a group document, taking the idea of the Lausanne Covenant and writing a local version. Agree together on the challenges around you and the behaviour that is consequently demanded of Christians living in your context.

Go further

- The C.S. Lewis institute offers a good introduction to making a personal 'rule of life', which it describes as 'an intentional pattern of spiritual disciplines that provides structure and direction for growth in holiness'. You can find it online.[18]
- Richard Foster's book *Freedom of Simplicity* argues that 'it is obligatory upon us to help one another hammer out the shape of Christian simplicity in the midst of modern affluence'. Foster goes on to discuss the danger of 'turning any expressions of simplicity into a new legalism'.[19] Discuss these quotations in a group or, if you can obtain a copy of the book, read chapter 7.

24

When the ne'er-do-well did well

Read: Luke 7:36–50

When the Pharisee who had invited him saw this, he said to himself, 'If this man were a prophet, he would know who is touching him and what kind of woman she is—that she is a sinner.' Jesus answered him, 'Simon, I have something to tell you' (vv. 39–40).

Consider

There is a rule of business in Hollywood that 'you are only as good as your last picture'. If you want to stay on the scene, you have to remain successful (and this often means financially successful). If your last film was a flop, appealing to previous successes is a thin argument. You must maintain your shine if you want to stay among the stars.

Prisoners in rehabilitation programmes live by very different slogans. One of them is 'You are better than your worst mistake.'[20] In a community full of people who have made serious mistakes, the challenge for the individual is *not* to be defined by what they have done. In positive prison activities, inmates are given opportunities to prove that they can do well when it matters.

The passage from Luke 7 brings together two people from very different backgrounds. One of them is Simon. As a Pharisee, he would have upheld the law in exacting detail. He possesses a certain status; he has the confidence to invite Jesus to dinner, at least. During the meal, a character from the gutter approaches. She is a known ne'er-do-well, the sort of person whose past enters the room with her.

Simon points out the sort of person she is, that her presence is a pollutant, that she doesn't belong in the company of religious achievers (v. 39). Jesus replies that, whatever mistakes the woman may have made, today she has got it right. She has washed him, kissed him and anointed him, with a heart full of love and a longing for redemption (vv. 44–47). Simon is put in the shade; it is the woman who takes the star turn. The prisoner's slogan has eclipsed Hollywood's and the moment is precious. In the parallel passage in Mark's Gospel, Jesus announces that 'wherever the gospel is preached throughout the world, what she has done will also be told, in memory of her' (Mark 14:9).

Write

You can take this theme in one of two directions for your journalling. If you are doubting yourself or feeling unsuccessful, recall the times when you have got something right, the moments you can point to and say, 'I did well then.' Often we forget these moments, especially when we are hard pressed and just want to move on to the next job that needs doing. But if the divine memory holds on to these gems, so should we.

Alternatively (or additionally) you can use your journal to work through your feelings about someone else. Bring to mind the people you find most difficult and unlovable. Make a note of their failings but don't go into detail (note that all Luke says about the woman in verse 37 is that she 'lived a sinful life'). Then, alongside your first notes, try to remember these people's better moments, when they acted well or longed for something good.

Share

Ask someone you trust for their recollection of a time when you got something right. It may be different from your own reckoning. If you are in a journalling group and know each other fairly well, you might start with this exercise. You could also focus on verses 41–43 and discuss the 'note on the passage' below.

Go further

- Make a list of things you have got right today (if you are journalling in the evening) or yesterday. Do you tend to forget moments that you would do well to hold in memory?

A note on the passage

A bewildering implication of this passage is that the more a person has sinned, the greater are the possibilities for them to respond to Jesus. The commentator John Nolland writes that 'there is no disagreement with the Pharisees about the sinfulness of Jesus' intimates, but he proposes a much more creative manner of dealing with this fact'.[21]

25

A moment of ease

Read: Acts 16:11–15

On the Sabbath we went outside the city gate to the river, where we expected to find a place of prayer (v. 13)

Consider

During one of his films, James Bond will go through a lot. Being chased, attacked, betrayed, intimidated, kidnapped and tortured are all par for the course. Even in a fictional adventure film, however, the action cannot be relentless. Neither the audience nor the hero can be expected to cope if the pressure never lets up. There must also be scenes where Bond is safe—receiving his briefing from Q, for instance, or exchanging the customary banter with Miss Moneypenny. Without an occasional change of pace, the film would be overwhelming for everyone.

The book of Acts is an adventure of a different kind. All the same, the apostles endure a great deal of hostility. The civic authorities regularly imprison them; they often have religious adversaries on their tail; even the weather stands in their way. In 2 Corinthians 11:23–28, the apostle Paul gives a comprehensive summary of his ordeals. Reading through Acts, you can see his point: there is a desperate situation around almost every corner.

Almost. From time to time, Luke gives respite to his readers, just as God gives breathing space to his followers, and there are episodes of blessed relief. One of these is in Acts 16. The scene is one of calm and safety, a place of prayer by a river on a sabbath day (v. 13). For once, there is no confrontation. Paul and his fellows can even sit down for a while. The group of God-fearing women they meet not only accept their message but offer further hospitality (v. 15). As chapter 16 continues, Paul and Silas are plunged back into the action of Acts, although it is interesting that they later return to Lydia's house (v. 40), presumably glad to know of a place where they can catch their breath.

Write

In verse 13, Paul and friends go to a place where they expect to find godliness and peace. In your journalling today, identify the people and places you know you can go to when you need a break from the action. Just as Acts 16 records the details of the sabbath and the river, call to mind the details that make your retreat spaces special and the hospitable touches that put you at ease. Write in a poetic style if you wish, perhaps focusing on a particular time when you were given respite from a pressured situation.

When you have finished, give thanks to God for the people and places you have journalled about, and consider when you will visit them next.

Share

Ask members of a journalling group to bring photos of their favourite places of rest and prayer, and begin a meeting by exhibiting the pictures. Ask also if anyone has experienced a time when they were hard-pressed and there was no relief—or did it turn out that, even at such a time, there was some sort of quiet support not too far away?

When you have done the journalling exercise, share your experiences with each other. As you do so, be sure to mention the homely details that made these times special.

Go further

- Look through Acts to find other 'moments of ease' amid the turmoil. Look also at the parts of Paul's letters (for instance, Romans 15:30–33) where the apostle's willingness to struggle for the gospel is balanced by his awareness that he needs refreshment.
- Make a playlist of music that you find calming, encouraging or uplifting. Have it ready for when you need it next.

A note on the passage

It is possible that the 'place of prayer' in Acts 16:13 was outside the city, because Roman legislation excluded unsanctioned religions from the urban precinct. It is ironic, then, that this was where Paul and his party found acceptance and where the mission to Philippi was begun. Equally, though, the river was a likely place of calm and cleansing, and may have been the ideal spot for Lydia's baptism (v. 15).

26

Credal crescendo

Read: Romans 8:31–39

Who shall separate us from the love of Christ? (v. 35).

Consider

Rhetorical questions can be very effective in a speech. Winston Churchill, one of the great speech-makers, frequently used them. During one of his first addresses in the House of Commons, he challenged a sharp rise in government spending in the following manner:

Has the wealth of the country doubled? Has the population of the Empire doubled? Have the armies of Europe doubled? Is the commercial competition of foreign nations so much reduced? Are we become the undisputed master in the markets of the world? Is there no poverty at home? Has the English Channel dried up, and are we no longer an island? Is the revenue so easily raised that we do not know how to spend it?[22]

Of course, there was no doubt about the answers to these questions. That is how rhetorical questions work, drawing the listener in and forcing the realisation that there is really only one answer. The person who asks such questions is, ironically, quite sure of their position.

The apostle Paul was another fine rhetorician, and Romans 8 is a chapter to read aloud with a flourish. Verses 31–35 are a crescendo of rhetorical questions. They roll in like waves and the argument rises, culminating in the final question, 'Who shall separate us from the love of Christ?' Then the dam bursts, and Paul can contain himself no longer. 'For I am convinced...' he now declares, and continues with his stirring creed of Christ's love. He wields his whole oratorical skill as he wrestles to persuade others of what he so passionately believes himself.

Write

Identify something in which you hold a strong belief, whether an aspect of Christianity (as with Paul) or something relating to society or politics (as with Churchill). Journal your feelings about this cause, and express the strength of your emotion by using a little rhetoric (including rhetorical questions). Aim to revisit your writing at a later stage to see how potent your argument sounds.

Share

Since rhetoric is generally written with an audience, if not a performance, in mind, try to read your journal piece out loud, and perhaps ask a friend to listen. This is easily arranged, of course, if you are working in a journalling group.

Group members might also discuss whether, in situations where you are explaining Christianity to someone else, you are inclined to press your point (as Paul does in Romans) or favour a quieter approach.

Go further

- Modern-day orators are worth watching for their ability to turn ideas and beliefs into an enthralling performance. Prime ministers, presidents and preachers are all exponents of the art: look for their speeches online.
- Browse through the epistles, looking for further examples of rhetorical flair.
- Consider how these thoughts on presentation might make a difference to the reading of scripture and the delivery of sermons in your church or fellowship.

A note on the passage

In verses 35 and 38–39, Paul is using another rhetorical technique—a climactic list: 'Neither death nor life, neither angels nor demons, neither the present nor the future, nor any powers, neither height nor depth, nor anything else in all creation, will be able to separate us...'. Churchill used this technique to similar effect in his famous words, 'We shall fight on the beaches, we shall fight on the landing grounds, we shall fight in the fields and in the streets, we shall fight in the hills...' This is another effect that you can try in your own writing.

27
Letting fly

Read: Galatians 5:7–12

As for those agitators, I wish they would go the whole way and emasculate themselves! (v. 12).

Consider

Sometimes people wonder whether they are allowed to take issue with anything in church. In a denunciation of what he terms 'The Cult of Nice', the priest and writer Justin Lewis-Anthony has this to say about the inability of church members to enter into open debate:

> It is as if conflict, or even disagreement, is never permitted in the Christian fellowship, by the very nature of that fellowship. Therefore, we tell ourselves, because we are not susceptible to conflict, we need do very little to learn from conflict.[23]

The letter to the Galatians is evidence that the early church did not suffer from this sort of reticence. Paul has genuine objections to what has been going on in this local church and does not tiptoe round any issues. 'I am astonished...' he snaps from the outset (1:6), and goes on in chapter 5 to attack those who have interfered with the Galatians' theology and have persuaded them that they need to observe old covenant regulations such as circumcision. If he is annoyed with the church for listening to this false teaching, he is even more annoyed with the false teachers and is not afraid to say so. 'I wish they would go the whole way and emasculate themselves!' he concludes, rather memorably.

For those of delicate sensibilities, it is a bit of a shock to find a verse like this in the Bible, but Paul's words cut right through the 'cult of nice'. Conflict and confrontation can be necessary, even productive. Paul feels no shame in revealing the strength of his feelings; perhaps we have something to learn from him.

Write

Take something of the free expression that Paul demonstrates and employ it in your own journalling. If there is anything that has been frustrating you, spell it out. Allow yourself the space to write what you really feel. Notice that behind Paul's tirade is his desire for the Galatian church to do better; indeed, they had previously been 'running a good race' (v. 7), and Paul clearly believes that they can do so again. Examine what lies behind your frustrations and what better things you would like to see emerge from an unsatisfactory situation.

Share

You could begin a journalling group by playing a version of the television show *Room 101*. Go round the group and ask each person to name a pet hate from everyday life. Find out how much sympathy others feel for these frustrations. When you come to the journalling exercise, you could write about this pet hate or another issue that has come to mind.

It has to be said that, despite its shock factor, there is something witty and succinct about verse 12. In many ways, this short, sharp shock is more effective than a protracted whinge. Somewhere in your journalling, express your irritation using a one-liner in the same style, and share it with the group rather than reading out a long grumble.

At the end of the meeting, pray for the situations you have been writing about. Notice that Galatians is framed by invocations of grace and peace (1:3; 6:18), so try to finish on a similar note.

Go further

- Reflect on whether there are ever situations where you could be more direct with people. If you decide there is an issue that you need to talk to someone about straight away, pray for the right balance between openness and graciousness.
- Read some more of Justin Lewis-Anthony's critique of timorous church culture, which he traces to an idealised picture of the country parson George Herbert. As well as his book on the subject, there is a shorter article on the *Guardian* website (2 June 2009).[24]

A note on the passage

Galatians 5:12 shows a hint of 'Semitic hyperbole'—a Jewish tradition of colourful exaggeration to make a point. Other examples in the Bible include Matthew 18:8 (where Jesus recommends amputation of limbs to avoid sin) and Philippians 3:8, where Paul considers that, compared to knowing Christ, his previous glories are 'rubbish'. 'Rubbish' is a tame translation; the Greek word is a bit coarser!

28

Praise with attitude

Read: Psalm 150

Let everything that has breath praise the Lord (v. 6).

Consider

In the film *Sister Act*, an unfortunate series of events leaves Deloris, a club singer (played by Whoopi Goldberg), taking refuge in a convent. Deloris ends up leading the unpromising choir. During a scene where she listens to individual voices, she asks one nun to sing an A, which she does bashfully at first. When Deloris manages to get a much bolder sound out of the nun, she remarks, 'We call that an A with an attitude.' She tells the sisters, 'You have to put attitude in what you sing… this is not just quacking, this is rejoicing. You are singing *to the Lord.*' Needless to say, she goes on to transform the choir.

As you read Psalm 150, ask yourself with what sort of attitude it was intended to be sung. The psalmist becomes a kind of conductor, pointing to the different sections of the ensemble. 'Now—trumpets!' he yells. 'Harp and lyre, your turn! Singers—come on, *praise!*' Surely it isn't possible that any of this could be done without a heap of exuberance, an uprising of 'attitude'. Many a choirmaster has had to rouse their singers to do justice to words like Psalm 150. The sound of rejoicing has to be noisy, daring and free.

The commentator Walter Brueggemann writes:

In a certain texture of religion, perhaps sponsored mainly by librarians, it may be proper to 'let all the earth keep silent'... Israel's characteristic way, however, is to... 'make a joyful noise'. There is something intrinsically boisterous, and from a certain perspective disordered and disruptive, about Israel's praise, eschewing, as it does, docility, passivity, and too much pious reverence.[25]

Write

Think about the times and places where you have ignored your 'inner librarian' and allowed your heart and mouth to sing praise with attitude. Make a list of these occasions in your journal and recall how you felt. Make a further list of places and gatherings where you know you can be, in your own way, lively and joyful. Thank God for all these things.

You can turn these lists into a song of your own in the style of Psalm 150. If you feel stirred both at the coast and in church, for example, then your psalm could go something like 'Praise him from the cliff tops and in the congregation.'

Share

There are various way to introduce this topic in a journalling group. You could watch some scenes from *Sister Act* together. You could try reading out Psalm 150 in different styles, from straight-laced to Pentecostal preacher (the latter works much better!). Depending on where you are meeting, you could even take a verse each and see who can read theirs with the most attitude.

Opening exercises like this should warm you up and loosen you up. Once you have written your own psalms of praise, take it in turns to read them out. Make sure you are not just quacking, but rejoicing!

Go further

- Look elsewhere in the Bible for evidence that Israel's praise is 'intrinsically boisterous'. Luke 19:37–40 (Jesus' triumphal entry into Jerusalem) and 2 Samuel 6:14–22 (David's dance in front of the ark of the covenant) are a start.
- Christian musical traditions have reflected the enthusiasm of Psalm 150 in various ways, from the gospel music featured in *Sister Act* through rousing hymns such as 'Praise to the Lord, the Almighty' to Matt Redman's 'Let everything that has breath'. Spend some time listening to these different expressions of praise.

29

Mottos and ditties

Read: 2 Timothy 2:8–13

Here is a trustworthy saying...(v. 11).

Consider

One of the features of social media is 'linking'. On blog pages or social networking sites, a user can direct their friends or followers to an article they find inspiring, a song from their childhood, a classic movie moment or any number of snippets that they think other people should know about as well.

The idea of linking was around long before the digital age and can be found in some surprising places, including the Bible. Paul's letters contain a number of song excerpts, such as the lines found in 2 Timothy 2:11–13. These words may have been known in the first-century church as a hymn. Paul 'links' to them at this point as they have something valuable to say about labouring and living for Jesus, a strong theme in his letter. He also includes some memorable mottos, such as his one-line 'gospel' (v. 8) and the upbeat quip 'God's word is not chained' (v. 9).

Although Paul has a reputation for writing rather academic letters, it is worth remembering that he also embeds, or links in, these mottos, ditties and other memorable lines. This is the sort of popular content that reinforces his message, the catchy words that people go away repeating to themselves. This is how the early church's creativity has been preserved in the Bible, thanks to some very long-lasting links.

Write

What Paul does in his pastoral letters is something that you can do in your own journalling.

Before you put pen to paper, spend some time recalling some 'best bits' of Christian culture—nicely expressed lyrics, memorable sermon moments, classic works, perhaps even material you have created yourself. Then, beginning with the words, 'I have the strength to continue as a Christian because...', write about the things that keep you inspired to follow Jesus, just as Paul did in his letter to Timothy. As you journal, consciously include some of the mottos, lyrics and other connections that you remembered.

Share

Here are some questions that you can discuss at the start of a journalling group.

- What are the elements that make sermons, songs or hymns memorable?
- Where do you imagine Paul was sitting when he wrote 2 Timothy 2? What mood was he in? Do details like this affect the way you read the passage?
- If you had to choose a verse from this passage to put up on your wall, which would it be?

As you approach the journalling exercise, it is worth talking together about your personal highlights from Christian art and culture. You will probably find that one person's choices will help others think of their own.

If you blog or use a social networking site, share links to some of the websites you have spent time discovering for your journalling. Other people may enjoy them too. If you are in touch with someone who is new to Christianity or who needs encouragement, consider sharing a link to something they might find beneficial.

Go further

- Look through Paul's letters and find other sayings and song fragments that he has included. (In many Bibles they are easy to spot because of the way they are laid out on the page, in verse form.)
- In Nick Hornby's novel *High Fidelity*, the narrator is a record shop owner and sometime DJ trying to get to grips with his love life. He constantly makes reference to songs, films and 'top five' lists: this is what helps him to understand himself and the people around him. It is an interesting example of a story that feeds on cultural titbits.

A note on the passage

2 Timothy demonstrates both the limitations and the oppor- tunities of having an ancient letter preserved for us to read. Although we know that Paul was a prisoner and seems to be in Rome as he writes (see 1:17), we don't have any further details. On the other hand, we do have here a vivid slice of the early church's conversation. As anyone who has looked

back over a journal will know, it is fascinating to review what an individual was thinking and feeling at a given moment in the past.

30
Robust definitions

Read: Hebrews 11:1

Now faith is confidence in what we hope for and assurance about what we do not see.

Read: Hebrews 6:19

We have this hope as an anchor for the soul, firm and secure.

Read: 1 John 3:16

This is how we know what love is: Jesus Christ laid down his life for us.

Consider

The environment in which the epistles were written was not always hospitable to Christianity. There were rival philosophies and political opponents in abundance. Yet despite this—indeed, because of this—the early church was keen to mark out its faith. In places, this firmness of purpose expresses itself in robust definitions. One towering example is Paul's discourse on love in 1 Corinthians 13. 'Love is patient, love is kind,' he insists (v. 4), and he has in mind Jesus, the cross and the church as he writes. Elsewhere—for example, in Hebrews and 1 John—there are further definitions of faith, hope and love. They are chiselled and hardwearing words of catechism for use in the real world. Faith is 'assurance about what we do not see' (Hebrews 11:1), hope is 'an anchor for the soul' (6:19), and love is all about Jesus Christ (1 John 4:9–10).

In more recent times, writers have rediscovered the concentrated potential of definitions, sometimes writing whole books of them. The definitions in Ambrose Bierce's *The Devil's Dictionary* are satirical: a 'Christian' is explained as 'one who believes that the New Testament is a divinely inspired book admirably suited to the spiritual needs of his neighbour'.[26] Frederick Buechner's *Wishful Thinking* and *Whistling in the Dark* are thought-provoking collections in which a 'parable' is 'a small story with a large point', and 'repentance' is 'to come to your senses, not so much something you do as something that happens'.[27] These writers show that working towards definitions is still worthwhile. It is a way of probing our presumptions, of marking out the world a little more clearly.

Write

Write your own definitions in your journal as a way of understanding the world around you. Start by writing the following words in a left-hand column: 'kindness', 'praise', 'grace', 'surprise', 'treasure'. Then, in the right-hand column, write definitions of each of these words. Your definitions could be personal ('kindness' might be 'when my family do the washing-up without being asked'). They could be technical ('grace' might be 'God's goodness in the face of our sinfulness'). They could be satirical ('surprise' could be 'what my face must express when I open my Christmas presents, no matter what's inside').

Once you have got the idea, come up with your own list of words and spend some time thinking of your own quirky definitions that relate to life and faith.

Share

This can be an enjoyable exercise for a journalling group to do together. Once you have read the Bible verses, look at the way other writers have used definitions. As well as sharing definitions you have written, you could ask each other to define words. Try giving everyone a slip of paper and asking them to write a column of five words. Then shuffle the slips and distribute them at random, so that each person works on defining someone else's list.

If you come up with a few lines you are pleased with (whether by yourself or in a group), consider sharing your definitions on a social networking site, where other people may respond with their own material.

Go further

- Sometimes the easiest way to grasp an idea like 'joy' or 'gentleness' is to observe a person who exhibits these qualities. Look at the fruit of the Spirit in Galatians 5:22–23 and see if you can match each virtue to someone you know.

A note on the passage

As the early church spread into lands that were influenced by Greek culture, there was friction between two different ways of thinking. Greek dualist philosophy conceived of separate realms—one physical and ignoble (the scruffy world we can see and touch), and another loftier, although immaterial (an abstract plane of virtue). In contrast, Christians preached that truth, goodness and love were nearby, at ground level. They had witnessed these qualities walking and talking in the person of Jesus Christ. So when, in 1 John, 'love' is defined in terms of this person, it is a provocative point.

31

Refreshingly honest

Read: James 4:13–17

What is your life? You are a mist that appears for a little while and then vanishes (v. 14).

Consider

The NIV Bible says, 'You are a mist'. Other translations give 'You are like a puff of smoke' (GNB), 'You're nothing but a wisp of fog' (THE MESSAGE) and 'What is your life? It is even a vapour' (KJV). However you read it, these are oddly disconcerting words. Elsewhere in the New Testament letters, believers are reassured of their identity, their destiny and their worth in God's eyes. Why these severe words from James?

In the liturgy for the beginning of Lent, the words of Genesis 3:19 are spoken to each individual as a cross of ash is traced on the forehead: 'Remember that you are dust, and to dust you will return.' These, too, are disconcerting words, but this is where Lent must start—admitting our mortality before God and not imagining ourselves to be more than we really are. It is a cold shower of honesty, a wake-up call to reality.

It is this kind of honesty that James is looking for in his letter. He is speaking to people who reckon themselves worldly-wise, people with plans and prospects. But only God is wise enough to know about plans and prospects, and the only sensible way of facing the future is to live in a humble relationship with the one who can help us. It might be a shock to hear, 'You are a mist', but, just as a good friend will be prepared to tell us an unwelcome truth, James is telling us something that ought to get our heads straight.

Write

If we can be honest about our mortality, we can go on to be honest about all sorts of things—our status, our appearance, our talents, our plans, our habits, our time of life, our achievements. In your journalling, begin with 'I am a mist'. Then write further statements about yourself that are unavoidably true (use a poetic form if you like). Try not to feel sorry for yourself in any of this, but keep in mind the focus of James 4:6: 'God opposes the proud but shows favour to the humble.' When you have finished, you should feel as if you have been refreshingly honest with yourself and God, and you may like to spend some time in silence or prayer.

Share

Being honest with each other in a journalling group may come naturally or feel difficult, depending on your person-alities and how well you know each other. You could begin by going round the group, each person completing the sentence 'If I'm honest, I have to admit...' Keep this exercise reasonably light-hearted.

When you have all completed the journalling exercise, read out only the parts that you feel comfortable sharing. In fact, you may find other people identifying with your self-assessment or challenging you if you are being too hard on yourself.

Go further

- Poetry is an arena in which writers can often address the uncomfortable issue of mortality. Death is a frequent theme in Shakespeare's sonnets (see, for instance, Sonnet 60: 'Like as the waves make towards the pebbled shore / So do our minutes hasten to their end'). 'To Autumn' by John Keats is a bittersweet anticipation of life's conclusion, while John Donne's 'Death, be not proud' faces down death with the consolation of faith. Look at some similar poems like these and consider which you find most moving—those that are strikingly stark or those that offer consolation.
- Alain de Botton's book *Status Anxiety* recognises the desperation of trying to get on in the world and offers a chapter on Christianity as a solution to this problem. It also includes a summary of Tolstoy's cautionary tale *The Death of Ivan Ilyich* and discusses the valuable tradition of *memento mori*.[28]
- Psalm 39:4–7 has many parallels with James 4, while keeping hold of faith and hope in God. You might like to read these words as a conclusion to your journalling.

32

Imagine how it will go

Read: 1 Peter 3:13–22

Always be prepared to give an answer to everyone who asks you to give the reason for the hope that you have (v. 15).

Consider

'Be prepared' is the well-known international motto of the Scout movement. When Robert Baden-Powell originally proposed it, he explained what he meant by it: a readiness both of mind and body, anticipating difficulties and obstacles and having the resources to deal with anything. These two words sum up much of the organisation's proactive ethos.

Reflection 31 noted the warning in James 4:13–14 that it is unwise to presume that plans will turn out as we expect. ('You do not even know what will happen tomorrow,' protests James.) Today's reading from 1 Peter is the balancing argument. Peter does not imagine that he or any other church member has a secure future (and, indeed, the early years of the church were turbulent). However, he realises that it is possible to think ahead, to be expectant in mind, body and spirit for whatever is around the corner. There may be suffering to come, but, Peter insists, we should remember that there is no shame in suffering for a good cause (vv. 14a, 17). There may be intimidation, but hold your nerve (v. 14b).

There may be questions, so have your answers to hand and 'be prepared' (v. 15).

Peter's words—the words of an elder to a young church—are at once reassuring and enlivening. 'Do not be surprised at the fiery ordeal that has come on you,' he says later (4:12), and the mere fact that a hardened old apostle regarded tough times as good and normal would have heartened many who weren't used to the idea. Meanwhile, the alert senses, the readiness for anything—the instincts of a spiritual Scout, we might say—would have set an example for the whole church.

Write

If possible, do this journalling exercise first thing in the morning or, if not, the night before, as you anticipate a new day. Imagine how things will go. Write down the situations that you expect to be difficult, what you think you will be up against. Where will you have to be careful? What difficult questions might you face? Where will your faith come into play and when might it be tested? Will any of your tasks be physically exacting? Try to journal the possibilities with the same resolve that Peter seems to have had.

Come back to your journal at the end of the day or at a later stage, and see how accurate your predictions were. Even if you didn't guess everything correctly, did you find that there was a value in being consciously prepared?

Share

There are a couple of ways to approach this exercise in a journalling group. You could spend time together sharing and journalling your expectations for the next day (or even the next week), and then, at your subsequent meeting, let each other know what actually happened and how you coped. Alternatively, agree to complete the whole exercise individually in advance of your meeting, so that you can discuss the results when you convene.

Go further

- Look at the Scout promise, law and motto.[29] See if they still make sense if you replace the word 'Scout' with the word 'Christian' or even 'A member of our fellowship'. Consider writing an alternative promise, law and motto for yourself or for your group.
- The use of the second person is reckoned to be the least common narrative voice. Most stories are told in the first person ('This is what happened to me, to us') or the third person ('This is what happened to him, to her, to them') and in the past tense. This is true in the Bible. The Old Testament chronicles, the Gospels and Acts generally use third-person narrative (or occasionally first person, as in Acts 20—21). The epistles, however, are different. They use the second person, they clarify the present and they anticipate the future. One example of this is in 1 Peter 3:21, which says, 'This water symbolises baptism that now saves you.' The effect is striking and personal. Try some creative writing of your own, using the second person to tell a story from the angle 'This is what will happen to you...'

33

An enigmatic cast list

Read: 3 John

I wrote to the church, but Diotrephes, who loves to be first, will not welcome us... Demetrius is well spoken of by everyone—and even by the truth itself (vv. 9, 12).

Consider

The cast list at the beginning of a play script has a function, introducing the names of the characters and perhaps what they do for a living. Occasionally, however, there is a little more detail, giving clues about the play. The *dramatis personae* for Shakespeare's *A Midsummer Night's Dream*, for instance, tells us who is in love with whom, and it's clear that the situation is complicated. *The Tempest* includes some immediately intriguing people: 'Gonzalo, an honest old counsellor', 'Caliban, a savage and deformed slave' and 'Ariel, an airy spirit'.

The characters in the brief epistle of 3 John are just as intriguing. There is Gaius, who is 'progressing spiritually' (v. 2). There is the unsavoury Diotrephes, who 'loves to be first' (v. 9). Perhaps most enigmatically of all, there is Demetrius, who 'is well spoken of by everyone—and even by the truth itself' (v. 12). Who were these people? What were they like? What had they said? How had they behaved? What do the remarks about them refer to? We cannot know the answers, but as we read this letter today, it is almost more interesting because we don't know precisely who these people were. We are left to fill in the gaps; we instinctively try to picture what went on among this first-century church cast. Their idiosyncrasies may even remind us of some people we know.

Write

Writing your own cast list can be an entertaining exercise. List some acquaintances—people at church or a circle of friends. Beside each name write a short phrase to describe that person (it can be as enigmatic as you like). As you do so, reflect on your relationships with these people, on their roles and their relationships with each other, and on God's relationship with them.

Making a cast list can also be a way into fiction. Try this as a creative exercise. Put together a list of intriguing characters and imagine how they would interact in a story.

Share

Creating a cast list works well as a group exercise. If you are all members of the same church or community, think of the local characters who stand out, and do your journalling together, describing the various roles that each person has. Alternatively, everybody could write a description of the most colourful church character they have ever met. You can then read these aloud and decide what would happen if these people were all locked in a church together.

3 John contains an instruction to imitate what is good (v. 11). Which characters around you are setting a noteworthy example for others to follow?

Go further

- If you are feeling brave, ask one or two people you trust to write a short description of you and how you fit into your church or community.
- Spend some time praying for important relationships around you.
- Have a look at Acts 17:1–15, where some of Paul's hearers are of 'noble' and some of 'bad' character. How do you feel about categorising people in this way yourself? Paul himself was never indifferent: he was loved or loathed by other people, and other people delighted or disgusted him. Is this a good way for a Christian to be?
- If you have access to the archives of a church or the local history section in a library, dig out some old parish magazines or records of events. Look out for colourful characters and telling remarks, and see what you can discover about the way things used to be.

34

Candid and contrite

Read: Psalm 51

For I know my transgressions, and my sin is always before me. Against you, you only, have I sinned and done what is evil in your sight (vv. 3–4).

Consider

Augustine's *Confessions* is reckoned to be the first autobiography in Western literature. Despite being a bishop in the church, educated and from a well-regarded family, he holds nothing back in his account of his own follies and shortcomings. Lust, theft and struggles with faith are all mentioned with remarkable honesty. Augustine seems to have swallowed his pride and deliberately shared these things for the benefit of other people. In a later letter, he wrote:

> *Thus, my son, take the books of my* Confessions *and use them as a good man should—not superficially, but as a Christian in Christian charity. Here see me as I am and do not praise me for more than I am... And if something in me pleases you, here praise Him with me—Him whom I desire to be praised on my account and not myself... Indeed, we were ourselves quite lost; but He who made us, remade us.*[30]

Psalm 51 is attributed to David, the king of Israel, and the psalm's heading gives the context: this is David's plea for forgiveness after the notorious episode in which he stole a wife and despatched the husband for good measure (more lust and theft, plus murder). Although the tone of the psalm is personal (it is written in the first person, for instance), the phrasing is general enough to have been included in Israel's hymn book as a confession that could be used by others in different circumstances. Indeed, parts of this psalm are frequently used as words of penitence in church services.

Making a confession is a vulnerable action. David and Augustine have no nobility for us to admire here, only humility. Their daring cry, to God and to others, is, 'Here see me as I am.' They hope that by being candid and contrite they will find sympathy and forgiveness, and will turn others towards God in the process.

Write

For today's journalling exercise, write a confession of your own. Follow the example of Psalm 51 and make your words general enough to be used again in a different situation, even if they are prompted by specific events that you are sorry for. Recognise, as David did, the sin that is always before you (v. 3); recognise also God's character and his willingness to forgive (v. 17). In the latter part of the psalm, David says what he would like God to do for him now and for Israel in the future (vv. 10, 12, 18). You might like to do something similar.

Share

Psalm 51 includes many treasured verses and phrases. If you are working in a group, spend some time discussing which verses you especially like.

When you have completed the journalling exercise, share phrases and sentiments from your own confessions that you feel have encapsulated what you want to say to God with particular effectiveness. If your confession is worded in such a way that any contrite Christian could use it, it need not include details that make you feel uncomfortable.

You could finish your time together by saying all or part of Psalm 51, praying for forgiveness as a group, or simply sitting together in silence.

Go further

- Like Psalm 51, Augustine's *Confessions* (AD398) contains a number of familiar and treasured phrases, including the words in the opening chapter, 'You have made us for yourself, and our hearts are restless until they find their rest in you.' Browse through some of the book to get a flavour of it (you can find translations on the internet).
- Gregorio Allegri's plaintive choral piece *Miserere Mei, Deus* uses the Latin text of Psalm 51. You could listen to it for pleasure or during a time of prayer and reflection.

A note on the passage

Reflection 7, 'Understanding envy', looked at the spoiled relationship between David and Saul after 'the Spirit of the Lord had departed from Saul' (1 Samuel 16:14). Some commentators read Psalm 51:11 ('Do not cast me from your presence or take your Holy Spirit from me') as David's desperate plea to avoid a similar end.

35

A tangle with time

Read: John 7:1–10

Jesus told them, 'My time is not yet here; for you any time will do'
(v. 6).

Consider

H.G. Wells wrote *The Time Machine* in 1895, just eight years
before the Wright brothers' historic flight. It was a time when
the progress of technology suggested that humankind might
soon develop mastery over all kinds of elements that were
previously uncontrollable. In fact, the book opens with an
after-dinner discussion on this topic. As the guests discuss
what sort of travel is possible and what is impossible, the
Time Traveller repeatedly challenges their preconceptions.

A civilised man… can go up against gravitation in a balloon,
and why should he not hope that ultimately he may be able to
stop or accelerate his drift along the Time-Dimension, or even
turn about and travel the other way?

The Time Traveller has invented a machine that allows
him to do this. It transpires, however, that he is far from in
control. Time travel itself is alarming, his adventures in the
world of the future are bewildering, and the vision of what

will become of humanity and the earth is harrowing. Control over time, we discover, is hardly control over providence.

Before his resurrection, Jesus was as limited by time and space as any other human being. He had a way with time, however, which came not from control but by being acutely aware of his Father's pace. In John 7, there is a practical reason why Jesus believes that the time is wrong for a grand appearance: the Jewish leaders are hunting for him (v. 1). There is also a spiritual dimension to it. Jesus senses the cataclysm gathering around him that will end with the cross, and his is a long view when he says 'My time is not yet here' (v. 6). There is no room for the impatience of his brothers, for whom 'any time will do'. A divine plan is unfolding, and it must move at the right speed.

Write

Jesus' concern to find the right time for everything is a lesson to anyone who has ever tried to move things on or squeeze them in (and, indeed, to anyone who has wished their life away or let opportunities drift). Take note of your attitude to time and comment on it in your journal. Has your life been moving at the right speed? Have you been itching to get on with an activity, or ignoring one, that might require heavenly timing? Have you detected any tensions between God's pace and the world's? Can you look back on any situations where the timing was perfect?

If you are using this reflection at the beginning of Holy Week, take stock of the pilgrimage of days that lies before you. Ask yourself whether there are particular aspects of Jesus' story that you want to concentrate on, and how you will give time to worship, prayer and reflection.

Share

It is good to remember that time and opportunity are God-given, including times of Christian fellowship. Given the topic, it might be apt to begin a journalling group in prayer, thanking God that this time is available and asking that it will be in some way holy for everyone attending.

For a warm-up exercise, go round the group asking everyone to relate an incident in their lives where the timing was either perfect or terrible. Go on from there to the reflection and journalling exercise above, and then share some of what you have written.

Go further

- John's Gospel is an account of Jesus waiting for a very particular 'hour'. Look through John 2:4; 8:20; 12:23–28; 13:1 and 17:1. Trace the progress from 'not yet' to 'now', a background thread that Jesus always seems to be keeping in mind.
- Many classic stories, from Greek tragedies to theatrical farce, hinge on the peculiar timing of events. Browse some stories in which events happen in the nick of time, a second too late or at just the wrong moment. If you write stories, think about how you can employ timing in this manner.

A note on the passage

The Greek word *kairos* used in verse 6 means not simply 'time' but 'critical moment'. The Greek word for 'world' in verse 7 is *cosmos*. Even as Jesus shelters in a Galilean backwater, the choice of language suggests that he is at the centre of something momentous.

36

And it was night

Read: John 13:21–30

After he had said this, Jesus was troubled in spirit and testified,
'Very truly I tell you, one of you is going to betray me' (v. 21).

Consider

When they are troubled in spirit, people in positions of
leadership and responsibility often have few people to talk
to. Perhaps it's for this reason that some make their journal
their confidante. After Albert's death in December 1861,
Queen Victoria wrote, 'With what a heavy broken heart
I enter on a new year without him!' During the top-secret
'Manhattan Project', US President Truman told his diary, 'We
have discovered the most terrible bomb in the history of the
world.' After an attempt on his life, another president, Ronald
Reagan, noted simply that 'getting shot hurts'. The anguish of
these sentiments must have been magnified by the fact that
there were few people who would understand them.

At the end of supper with his disciples in John 13, Jesus
is troubled in spirit because he can see what is coming:
'one of you is going to betray me' (v. 21). All but one of his
disciples are stunned by this announcement (v. 22). Perhaps
they have a dim sense of what is going on around them, but
they are hardly bearing Jesus' burden with him. Jesus, for

his part, keeps many thoughts to himself. He doesn't tell his friends the grim meaning of his parting words to Judas (vv. 27–28). While the disciples remain in the dark, Jesus sees the full extent of the darkness. 'And it was night,' the passage concludes (v. 30); indeed, it is a very black hour.

A certain fortitude can sometimes be observed in lives clouded by the shadow of death. As Jesus urges Judas to get on with his inevitable business (v. 27), he seems as steadfast in his spirit as he is troubled.

Write

Choose one of these tasks for a journalling exercise:

* Write about a predicament of which only you know the full extent. 'Talk it over' with your journal if there are not many people with whom you can discuss the situation.
* When we read John 13, we know much more than the disciples did. We understand why Jesus was 'troubled in spirit'; we know what awaited him; we know that there was a plan of salvation in the background. Address Jesus as if in a letter, responding to him and giving thanks for what you now understand. If you like, read on into John 14—15 and write your own responses to some of the things Jesus says there. This exercise is particularly appropriate if you are journalling during Holy Week.

Share

There may be many personal issues in this journalling exercise that are best kept private. As always in a group, share what you can and respect any group member who would rather not share anything.

If you are meeting at the end of Lent, begin a group by sharing how life feels in general at the moment. Do you feel at odds or in tune with the heaviness of Holy Week?

You could also think about the confidences and pressures that leaders live with every day (giving rise to such expressions as 'It's lonely at the top'). Try to sympathise with such people rather than criticising them, and take some time to pray for them.

Go further

- Look at verse 2 of the hymn 'I cannot tell', which makes the point that there are elements of Jesus' suffering that we may understand and others that we may not. Use these words in a period of quiet reflection.

A note on the passage

'And it was night' (v. 30) is an example of what T.S. Eliot called an 'objective correlative', where we are given a clue about what is going on inside a person from a symbolic detail happening outside. There is another objective correlative in John 18:17–18, where Peter denies Jesus and 'it was cold'. This literary device reflects the fact that there are often connections between our emotions and our surroundings, something you might like to bear in mind when journalling.

37

Epigrams of doubt and faith

Read: John 18:33–38

'Everyone on the side of truth listens to me.' 'What is truth?'
(vv. 37–38).

Consider

Many writers have learned the value of epigrams—pithy sayings made powerful by their brevity (not far from the idea of 'soundbites'). Perhaps the most famous exponent of the epigram was Oscar Wilde. 'I can resist everything except temptation,' says one of his characters in the 1893 play *Lady Windermere's Fan*, and 'We are all in the gutter, but some of us are looking at the stars.'

The conversation between Jesus and Pontius Pilate in John's Gospel is a drama all of its own. There is something Wildean in the confrontation of wits, but this is no comedy of manners. The exchanges are snappy yet highly charged as they resound around the palace interior. Jesus speaks timeless words of faith: 'My kingdom is not of this world' (v. 36) and 'Everyone on the side of truth listens to me' (v. 37). Pilate's responses are laced with irony and doubt: 'You are a king, then!' (v. 37) and 'What is truth?' (v. 38). As readers, we decide whose view of things we like; we choose which epigrams we will take to heart.

Write

What one-liners of faith and doubt do you hear around you in the world today, about God, about human nature, and about what is happening to people? Divide a page in half and sketch out how voices for and against faith are confronting each other in our time. You may remember actual quotes that sum up a person's position, or you might assemble your own epigrams that typify a certain point of view.

You could develop this exercise further by imagining a modern-day debate about an aspect of Christianity. Write a curt, epigrammatic conversation between two characters, one speaking from faith and one from doubt or cynicism. It could take the form of either a script or a short story with dialogue.

Share

If you are doing this exercise with a group, begin by naming as many epigrams from film and literature as you can think of. Off the top of your head, can you think of parts of the Bible that are expressed tersely in order to make a point?

Share your one-liners of doubt and faith when you have written them; discuss how persuasive these voices are and whether or not the world is listening to them.

If anyone has written a dialogue, divide the parts between two people and try a dramatic reading. Attempting a piece of writing like this means coming up with both sides of the argument; talk about whether this is a useful or an unsettling experience.

Go further

- Look forward through John's account of Jesus' death and resurrection. If possible, use a version of the Bible that shows the words of Jesus in red print. Notice the many brief things that Jesus says, and how full of meaning they are—the single word 'Mary' (John 20:16) being the epitome.
- Find internet video clips of dialogues and debates between people such as Rowan Williams, Jonathan Sacks, Richard Dawkins, and Peter and Christopher Hitchens. Listen out for arguments that are neatly and succinctly put.

A note on the passage

In this fascinating exchange with Pilate, it is worth thinking about why, when Pilate asks if Jesus is the king of the Jews, Jesus responds, 'Is that your own idea?' (see vv. 33–34). Perhaps Jesus is avoiding a simple answer, because the nature of his kingship is so easily misunderstood. Perhaps he is probing to see whether the Roman governor has any glimmer of insight. Or perhaps he is effectively saying, 'You need to have your own opinion about me', something that the Gospel writer John would like all his readers to realise.

38
No reasoning with a crowd

Read: John 19:1–16

Once more Pilate came out and said to the Jews gathered there,
'Look, I am bringing him out to you to let you know that I find no
basis for a charge against him.' … As soon as the chief priests and
their officials saw him, they shouted, 'Crucify! Crucify!' (vv. 4, 6).

Consider

The problem that Pilate encounters during Jesus' trial is a
problem that every political leader has to face when making
decisions: a crowd may form ideas of their own that are
contrary to the leader's. 'I find no basis for a charge against
him,' says Pilate before showing Jesus to the crowd. But
the crowd are fixated and call for Jesus' death as soon as he
appears. There is no reasoning with them.

Public opinion is often easily swayed. In John 12, a crowd
is welcoming Jesus into Jerusalem. On that occasion, it is the
Pharisees who are frustrated that 'the whole world has gone
after him' (v. 19). It is not long, however, before they claim
to speak for everyone and Pilate cannot resist their demand
for Jesus' crucifixion.

The 2006 film *The Queen*, the story of the British monarchy's reaction to the death of Princess Diana, addresses the
topic of dealing with mass opinions. In the film, the Queen's

instinct is to remain private and removed: 'That's the way we do things in this country. Quietly. With dignity.' Eventually, though, the clamour of the crowd and the media for a more demonstrative royal reaction forces her hand. The woman who thought she knew the British public declares at the end of the film, 'I don't think I shall ever understand what happened this summer.' These could easily be the words of anyone who has had to deal with a crowd. Sometimes their reactions come as a total surprise.

Write

Throughout his ministry, Jesus set little store by public opinion, choosing instead to listen to his heavenly Father. The early church was also wary of the 'world', with its wayward anxieties and obsessions (see, for instance, Romans 12:2). A Christian point of view has always been sceptical of the crowd.

In your journalling, work through some questions about the crowds in your life. Who is 'the crowd' as far as you are concerned? How are you influenced by the crowd? How is the crowd right? How is it wrong? How can it be resisted when it is wrong? What can be done if, apparently, it cannot be resisted? How can you make sure that you hear God's voice and voices of reason as well as the voice of the crowd?

Share

If, during the course of your journalling, you discover that you have a strong and coherent opinion that goes against the general tide, consider writing it out in the form of a letter. You could keep the letter to yourself; alternatively, you could send it to a newspaper or other publication (an interesting exercise if you have never done it before).

You could introduce the theme in a journalling group by looking at a newspaper together. Look for the opinions that politicians hold, and for the public opinions they have to bear in mind. Look also at opinion columns and the 'Letters to the Editor' page.

You might also conduct an experiment in peer pressure. Place a bar of chocolate on a table in the middle of the group, and choose one person who has to resist the urge to eat some. Throughout your meeting, all the other group members should try to persuade this person to take a bite. At the end of the meeting, ask the person what the experience felt like.

In between these activities, share what you have journalled in the usual way. It can be revealing to hear about the various groups that people feel are influential.

Go further

- Crowds are not always bad things: they can create infectious energy. Make a list of the best experiences you have had as part of a crowd.
- There are several paintings and sculptures entitled *Ecce Homo* (Latin for 'Here is the man', from John 19:5). Find some of them online and think about what makes them striking.

39

Stripped-down sorrow

Read: John 19:16–27

*There they crucified him, and with him two others—one on each
side and Jesus in the middle (v. 18).*

Consider

In 1986 the space shuttle *Challenger* exploded on live television. The footage is as shocking to watch now as it was at
the time. In some ways it is worse if you have seen it before.
As the shuttle rolls on to its back and the sky darkens, you
know what is coming.

The NASA commentary during the event was curiously
unemotional. As the shuttle launched, details of its veloc-
ity, altitude and position were relayed. Even as there was a
flash and smoke streaked in all directions, the commentator
seemed not to notice. Then there was a long pause. Eventually the voice returned with the same dispassionate tone:
'Flight controllers here looking very carefully at the situation. Obviously a major malfunction.' In a way, there was
nothing else to say. The disaster was clear for all to see. The
commentator had a job to do; he simply carried on doing it.

John's account of Jesus' crucifixion is remarkably un-
embellished. He, too, is a commentator who needs only to
present the facts. Jesus is crucified; the soldiers cast lots for

his garments; a disciple takes Jesus' mother into his home. Pilate is correspondingly brusque: 'What I have written, I have written,' he declares (v. 22), and that is the end of it. The whole business is told in a quiet, steady tone, with no comment on the horror or the misery of what happened. John's readers can work that out for themselves.

Sometimes a stripped-down style is the best way of presenting distressing events. Sometimes it is the only way a chronicler can manage to record them.

Write

Good Friday calls to mind the general brokenness of human experience. The cross is about Jesus' sacrifice for the sake of the world. At the same time it is a reminder of the sort of world that needs help, a world that is wretched and mortal. In your journalling today, face some of the difficult things that you have encountered, perhaps hard circumstances or strained relationships. Write about them in simple, stark terms, so that you have recognised and laid out the facts.

Once you have written your account, you may prefer to leave it at that. Spend some time just sitting with your experiences of our difficult and damaged world, so that you are aware of the many things that need redeeming. Use a holding cross if you have one.

Alternatively, you could finish your journalling by writing a prayer. Again, make it uncomplicated, naming what is wrong and asking for God's mercy. If you like, you could write your whole journal entry as a prayer of this kind.

Share

In a journalling group, look at the passage and compare it with another Gospel account of the crucifixion—for instance, Luke 23, where there is weeping, mocking, anger and dialogue. Discuss why you think John's description is more sparing. (Does he prefer not to dwell on Jesus' death? Is he intentionally leaving more to the imagination? Does his real interest lie less in the details and more in the significance of the cross?)

A way of sharing what you have journalled is to place a cross in the centre of the group and to lay your journals around the foot of the cross. People can place their journals open if they are happy for others to read what they have written, or closed if they would rather keep their thoughts private. Spend some quiet time reading what people have written and reflecting on the cross, and finish with prayer.

Go further

- There are a number of liturgies available for Good Friday. Browse some of them online.[31] Look for prayers that combine solemnity with simplicity.
- Find poems that appeal for a restrained reaction to death, such as Joyce Grenfell's 'If I should go' and Wendy Cope's 'My funeral'.

A note on the passage

There is great irony in Pilate's single-mindedness (v. 22). Having questioned what truth is and having given in to the crowd, he finally puts his foot down—although, of course, this action is far too late to be of any use. The inscription he refuses to alter does, in fact, proclaim a truth—that of Jesus' kingship. How far Pilate recognised this truth remains uncertain.

40

Out of the pit

Read: Psalm 40

He lifted me out of the slimy pit, out of the mud and mire… He put a new song in my mouth, a hymn of praise to our God (vv. 2–3).

Consider

It is true that there is a state of hope which belongs to bright prospects and the morning; but that is not the virtue of hope. The virtue of hope exists only in earthquake and eclipse… Exactly at the instant when hope ceases to be reasonable it begins to be useful.[32]

God can deliver. Israel had taken this belief to heart and passed it on through its stories, from Noah to the exodus to David and Goliath. Psalm 40 begins with this theme. Whatever pit we have fallen into, whatever slime we are stuck in, God's is the strong arm that can extract us (v. 2).

For all the consolation of God's help in the past, however, the problems of the present persist. From verse 11, the psalmist begins to reveal a heaviness of spirit. The faith that, in the first part of the psalm, seemed to bestow a relaxed confidence now becomes a desperate lifeline. 'You are my help and deliverer,' the psalmist concludes; 'you are my God, do not delay' (v. 17).

The psalm echoes our own often divided feelings. We have faith, but we also have trouble, and the two are in tension. Hope in God is not always a comfortable pillow on which we recline; sometimes it is more like a rope that we hang on to for dear life.

Perhaps this is never more true than when we confront our own mortality. There really is nothing, apart from God, that will get us out of this, and even believers may occasionally struggle with the idea of life resuming beyond death. Jesus' disciples certainly struggled with it: after Jesus' execution they simply locked themselves away (John 20:19). Whether any hope flickered in their hearts, we do not know for sure, but if it did it must surely have been of the desperate variety. As Psalm 40 testifies, there may be a hiatus between desolation and deliverance, during which all that God's people can do is to hang on. As Chesterton pointed out, however, this is when hope does its best work.

Write

What difficult matter do you need God's help with? What is the improbable future that you dare to hope for? How easy do you find it to hold on to hope? Call to mind your long-term longings and write about them in your journal. Record the hope that you have in the God of new songs and resurrection; but if the waiting is hard, mention that too. As you journal your thoughts, you could incorporate phrases from Psalm 40 that echo your own feelings (for example, 'None can compare with you'; 'Be pleased to save me, Lord'; 'Do not delay', vv. 5, 13, 17).

Share

As you come to the close of this journalling book, take a moment to step back and reflect on the experience. Ask yourself what you have learned and, looking through your journal, what progress you have made. If you have been journalling during Lent and are approaching Easter, ask yourself what wisdom and encouragement the season has brought.

If you are part of a journalling group, discuss these thoughts together. If you have been writing alone, consider whether there is anything arising from your journalling that you could usefully discuss in a fellowship group or with friends.

Go further

- Listen to a recording of U2's song '40', which is based on Psalm 40 and which the band often used to sing to finish their concerts.
- Read S.M. Lockridge's sermon 'Sunday's coming', which is particularly evocative in the time between Good Friday and Easter.[33]
- Read some famous epitaphs, such as the one that US statesman Benjamin Franklin wrote for himself, which face the reality of death while maintaining the hope of new life.[34]

A note on the passage

Throughout Psalm 40 there is a back-and-forth movement of covenant agreement between God and the psalmist. God has undoubtedly been faithful in the past (vv. 2, 5), just as the psalmist has kept his obligations to God (vv. 8–10). Now he petitions God to uphold him again (vv. 11, 13, 16–17). This process of calling on God's promises while fulfilling our own side of the bargain is the essence of Christian discipleship and a good focus for journalling.

Afterword

I hope that you have found your journalling rewarding as you have used this book. If this was your first taste of journalling as a spiritual discipline, it is worth thinking about where you will take it from here. Here are some suggestions to consider.

- **Evaluate your journalling:** Which reflections in this book really struck a chord with you? Which journalling activities were enjoyable and which were challenging? Did you enjoy variety and creativity, or did you gravitate towards a particular way of journalling? When was your journalling a delight and when was it hard work? Answering questions like these can help you think realistically about the focus and frequency of your future journal-keeping.
- **Keep your journalling fresh:** Maintaining a healthy and lasting appetite for journalling often depends on your approach to it. Journalling is a discipline, but it is marked by an essential freedom. Nobody is making you do it. There is no prescribed method or timetable that you must maintain. So do your journalling because it is nourishing, not because it is a duty. Remain open to new ideas that may reinvigorate your journalling from time to time. If you have enjoyed the element of creative writing in this book, continue to use your journal as a place to experiment with poetry and prose. Talk about your journal, especially with other journal-keepers.
- **Include the Bible in your journalling:** The implicit understanding in these reflections is that a Bible and a

journal are natural neighbours on a bookshelf. The 40 Bible passages included are just a sample of the many that can lead to fruitful journalling. If you continue to read the Bible as part of your journalling time, it may help in all sorts of ways. The Bible always introduces a 'voice from outside' into our train of thought, which can cut through stale or circular thinking, stave off the feeling that we have nothing to write about and, most of all, remind us of God. Remember that the Bible's authors were not so different from you. They, too, were journalling after a fashion, and for the same reason as you—to address life in the light of what God has done.

Suggested reading

On spiritual journalling

- Ron Klug, *How to Keep a Spiritual Journal* (Augsburg Fortress, 2002).
- Edward England (ed.), *Keeping a Spiritual Journal* (Highland Books, 1988).

On the Bible's writing

- David Winter, *The Bible Made Clear* (Lion, 2008).
- Leland Ryken, *Words of Delight: A literary introduction to the Bible* (Baker Academic, 1992).

Notes

1. R. Klug, *How to Keep a Spiritual Journal* (Augsburg Fortress, 2002), ch. 2.
2. The observation of Leland Ryken, a literary critic of the Bible. See *Words of Delight: a literary introduction to the Bible* (Baker Academic, 1992), p. 31.
3. C. Child, *Telling Ourselves in Ink: Creative Writing in the Church* (Grove, 2009).
4. From the essay 'The Poetic Principle', available online.
5. J. Goldingay, *Numbers and Deuteronomy for Everyone* (SPCK, 2010).
6. Book 2, chapter 10. Translated by W. Rhys Roberts.
7. A. Plass, 'Something beautiful', in *View from a Bouncy Castle* (Fount, 1991).
8. The Northumbria Community, *Celtic Daily Prayer* (Collins, 2005), p. 92. The quote is by Kate Tristram.
9. *Don Quixote*, Volume II, chapter VII. The translation is by John Ormsby and is available online.
10. B.G. Webb, *Five Festal Garments* (IVP, 2000), p.35.
11. S. Covey, *The 7 Habits of Highly Effective People* (Simon & Schuster, 1992), pp. 240–241.
12. See http://luhrmann.net and http://alumni.stanford.edu/get/page/magazine/article/?article_id=54818.
13. J. Oswalt, *Isaiah Chapters 40—66* (NICOT) (Eerdmans, 1998), p. 526.
14. David Runcorn, *Choice, Desire and the Will of God* (SPCK, 2003), p. 110.
15. C.S. Lewis, *Surprised by Joy* (Fount, 1977), p. 182.
16. Entry for July 15, 1944; from the Anne Frank Center website.
17. From section 9 of the Lausanne Covenant, 'The Urgency of the Evangelistic Task'. The Lausanne Covenant can be found at www.lausanne.org.
18. www.cslewisinstitute.org/webfm_send/338
19. R. Foster, *Freedom of Simplicity* (SPCK, 1981), p. 111–112.
20. See Joanna Jepson's article 'Freedom on death row', *Third Way* (Vol 36, no. 6), p. 24.

21. J. Nolland, *Luke 1—9:20* (Word Biblical Commentary) (Thomas Nelson, 2010), p. 356.
22. This and other speeches can be found at www.winstonchurchill.org.
23. J. Lewis-Anthony, *If You Meet George Herbert on the Road, Kill Him* (Mowbray, 2009), ch. 4.
24. www.theguardian.com/commentisfree/belief/2009/jun/02/george-herbert-anglican-vicar.
25. W. Brueggemann, *The Psalms and the Life of Faith* (Fortress Press, 1995), p. 114. The title of this chapter is 'A politics of glad abandonment'.
26. The text of *The Devil's Dictionary* is available online at www.thedevilsdictionary.com.
27. Frederick Buechner, *Wishful Thinking* (HarperCollins, 1993) and *Whistling in the Dark* (HarperSanFrancisco, 1994).
28. Alain de Botton, *Status Anxiety* (Penguin, 2005)
29. http://scouts.org.uk
30. 'Letter to Darius', translated by Albert C. Outler.
31. Good Friday liturgies can be found at www.churchofengland.org/media/41156/tspashw.pdf and http://onlineministries.creighton.edu/CollaborativeMinistry/stations.html
32. G.K. Chesterton, *Heretics* (John Lane, 1905), ch. 12. The text is available online.
33. Text available online at http://pasturescott.org/2007/04/10/sundays-comin.
34. See http://sln.fi.edu/franklin/timeline/epitaph.html.

Also by Corin Child

Hanging Out with Jesus

Six interactive Bible studies for 9–14s

Hanging out with Jesus provides an ideal framework in which to help young people in the church grow a sense of belonging and identity at a critical stage of their lives.

Aimed primarily at the 9–14 age group, each session begins by discussing the young people's own life experience. The six sessions then provide an overview of what being a Christian is all about, beginning with listening and then moving on to explore prayer, repentance, being a witness, and the extraordinary implications of Jesus' cross and resurrection.

Each session focuses on a New Testament character whose life was changed by the person they spent time with, and offers ideas for welcome, a prompt sheet for discussion, a Bible passage to explore, suggestions for quiet ways to reflect on the passage, and ideas for concluding either with a lively game or a reflective activity.

ISBN 978 1 84101 790 7   £8.99
Available from your local Christian bookshop or direct from BRF:
www.barnabasinchurches.org.uk